Creating Trump Nation

ISBN: 978-1-5136-1859-3
Cover Art: Dwayne Bassett
Internal Design: Colin Hawk

Printed in The United States of America

How blessed is the man who does not walk
in the counsel of the wicked,
Nor stand in the path of sinners,
Nor sit in the seat of scoffers!
But his delight is in the law of the Lord,
And in His law he meditates day and night (Psalm 1:1-2.)

Protesting to be wise, they became fools, and exchanged the glory of
the incorruptible God for an image in the form of corruptible man
(Romans 1:22-23a.)

Non-Fiction

Hi, My Name Is Jack, Simon and Schuster, 2011

Recovering from Religious Abuse, Simon and Schuster, 2011

We Believe: 30 Days to Understanding Our Heritage, Dunham Books, 2010

Real Prayers for Real People with Real Problems, Dunham Books, 2013

The Search for Reality, McGee and Me Publishing, 2015

Fiction

Full Moon Frenzy, 5 Moon Press, 2015

Spanish Moon Zephyr, 5 Moon Press, 2015

Snow Moon Queen, 5 Moon Press, 2015

Crescent Moon Darkness, 5 Moon Press, 2015

Blood Moon Judgment, 5 Moon Press, 2015

Unholy Seduction, 5 Moon Press, 2016

Feet of Clay, 5 Moon Press, 2017

Table of Contents

Introduction

Hi, my name is Jack Watts. I'm the person responsible for electing Donald J. Trump the 45th President of the United States, and I'm very proud of what I've done.

You heard me right. I got Trump elected. Well, not just me, obviously. There were millions of others who were also responsible. Collectively, we did it, and I'm going to show you "in real time" precisely how we accomplished this task.

While Hillary Rodham Clinton was spending $1.2 billion to win the election, Trump spent less than half that much. Yet, he won. It's because he dominated the most effective and influential tool of the campaign—my site and others like mine on Facebook. Best, it didn't cost him a dime, which I'm certain pleased the Trumpster very much.

You might ask, who do I think I am to make such a lofty claim? It's a fair question and deserves a straightforward answer.

I am a simple guy from Atlanta, Georgia—a patriot who loves his country. I'm also educated well enough to know a thing or two, and I have the ability to articulate what I believe effectively to others. I received my A.B. from Georgia State University in political science, my M.A. from Baylor University in Church-State Studies, and all but a dissertation for a Ph.D. in International Politics from Emory University. Finally, I'm an unapologetic born-again Christian.

But it wasn't my academic pedigree that was so helpful in gaining Trump's victory. It was the passion I have for the United States— my deep love and conviction that America can become great once again. Out of the depth of my heart, which is clearly pro-Trump and anti-Hillary, I posted thousands of times during the 2016 election.

Because my convictions are real and my words were genuine, my message resonated to thousands on Facebook, but it had nothing to do with the Republican Party. My Facebook friends and I are not partisan—not like the mainstream media would think anyway. We are motivated to action because of our beliefs, which are pro-American and Christian. Because Trump tapped into our values, we embraced him as a strong leader whose worldview mirrored ours. Because I wrote about this, I attracted many.

What I wrote influences a large following and generated an enormous response, but it all transpired under the radar. It also occurred in the heat of the battle, when people were developing their opinions about what was happening. It was this dynamic that made my comments more powerful than Hillary's ads—all of

which were focus group tested. They were stale—never spontaneous and heartfelt, like my posts were. The importance of this
cannot be overstated.

Although Hillary Clinton owned the mainstream media and its
cadre of sycophantic journalists—those who pursued a relent-
less attack against Donald Trump, calling him every name in the
book—I was equally fierce in my defense of what he was trying
to accomplish. The media thought they controlled the narrative
throughout America, influencing millions for Hillary, but they were
mistaken. They didn't. Maintaining this false assumption as much
as any other factor doomed Hillary's candidacy.

The media's negative message about Trump didn't resonate with
anybody other than the Far Left and those who were corruptible.
While they were castigating Trump as a narcissistic, womanizing
buffoon, people like me rejected their mean-spirited character as-
sassination. We refused to be distracted by their skewed narrative.

Instead of responding to the criticism, I chose to post about the
relevant issues of the campaign—our poorly run and over-regu-
lated economy, our weakened military, and the massive govern-
mental corruption that eats away at the soul of our nation. I also
posted frequently about Hillary Clinton's corruption and her responsibility for creating the mess we now have.

While the mainstream media filled the airways with ad hominem
attacks against Trump, seasoned with statements about the in-
evitability of a Progressive victory, they never realized they were

talking over the heads of most Americans. Because they have been successful in previous Presidential elections using this methodology, the pundits assumed they had the pulse of the nation, but they didn't. I did.

My efforts were truly grass-root, hitting a nerve with my readers repeatedly—an effort replicated by many others. The response to what I wrote was positive, and it grew steadily throughout the campaign. By the time the election was held, people from all over America looked to me for analysis, wisdom, and leadership. I was receiving thousands of hits a day on Facebook, as well as on Twitter at @hiJackwatts and on my We Believe America blog on Wordpress, where my Facebook messages were replicated. Unlike the mainstream media, who mistakenly believed people were being influential by them, my friends and followers definitely were being led by me.

My audience was real and it was loyal—fiercely loyal. Through thick and thin, we held together against the onslaught of the press, who condescendingly told us Hillary Clinton's victory was inevitable. Mockingly, the media assured us we were wasting our time supporting Trump, but we weren't. They said he couldn't win because he didn't have a ground game and Hillary did, but this definitely wasn't true. We were his ground game, and we connected daily in cyberspace to further his agenda. We were in constant and repeated communication with one another.

It wasn't all smooth sailing though. At times, it was very difficult, especially when the audiotape of Trump talking inappropriately surfaced. Since most of my Facebook friends are Christians, this was very hard, but we weathered the storm. Routinely, I responded to the media's attacks against Trump, telling my audience to hang tight, and it paid off. As difficult as it was, knowing the depth of Hillary's dishonesty, I consistently reminded my readers that a Clinton Presidency would be catastrophic for our beloved nation.

Instead of abandoning Trump, we doubled down with our resolve to get him elected. Defying all odds, while being mocked and vilified for our beliefs, we stuck together, becoming tied at the hip in cyberspace. We definitely became stronger each day because of the adversity we experienced, but it was also very exciting, fulfilling, and purposeful.

We are not racists because we support Trump. We are not misogynistic or xenophobic either. We are Americans and proud of it. We have never been ashamed of our nation, and we have never felt the need to apologize for being Americans. Why should we apologize? We are the beacon of hope for the entire world and have always been. It's why so many want to migrate here.

President Obama doesn't believe in America. It's obvious. It's why he has apologized for us repeatedly during the entire eight years of his Presidency. Just as bad, the media has fawned over him for behaving this way. Obama's Progressive followers might like this, but the rest of the country certainly does not. We resent it. We deeply resent it.

Obama has always been ashamed of us. If possible, Hillary is even worse. She has labeled us irredeemable and deplorable, and she meant what she said. To Barack and Hillary, being anti-American is the new patriotism. It's the cause they champion consistently.

This isn't how most Americans feel though, far from it. To us, their "enlightened patriotism" is decidedly unpatriotic, but what we think doesn't matter to Barack Obama or Hillary Clinton. To them, we are ignorant, unsophisticated, and unenlightened. We should remain silent and submissive to our superiors, meaning them.

Progressives, led by Barack Obama and Hillary Clinton, hold our beliefs in contempt. They ridicule us, belittling us for clinging to our guns and to our Bibles. They consistently look down on us, arrogantly believing they have a right to do so. Because they are enlightened and we are not, they are entitled to lead. This is also why they view us derisively, insisting that it is our responsibility to be subservient. It's our duty to submit to their superior worldview. This is precisely what they believe.

They expected us to acquiesce, but we refused. Most of us have had enough of them to last a lifetime. Being fed up, we rebelled against their leadership and their politically correct nonsense. We sent them packing, which is something they never expected— never in a million years.

Wearing their demeaning condemnation as a "Badge of Honor," people like me refused to kowtow to their erroneous belief system. Instead, we chose to fight back, knowing we would be called racist and misogynistic for doing so. We repudiated their anointed candidate, Hillary Clinton, knowing she is the most corrupt candidate to ever be nominated for the Presidency.

I spoke out against her consistently on Facebook, but rather than take cheap shots at her like the press was doing to Trump, I championed issues instead of caustic assaults. For the most part, I didn't engage in ad hominem attacks. Regardless of what the topic was, when I wrote, I always posted the truth. It made my credibility on Facebook increase substantially.

Although we opposed every one of Hillary's dishonest actions, our campaign wasn't simply opposition to her. It was also decidedly for Donald Trump and his commitment to make America strong again. His message resonated with us because we stand for America first, last, and always. It's who we are.

We oppose the globalism of Hillary, Barack Obama, and John Kerry. Their god is the state; ours is Almighty God. They loathe Christianity, while we fiercely embrace our Judeo-Christian heritage. We proudly champion the beliefs of our Forefathers and reject the historical revisionism of Obama, Hillary, and the Progressives. They champion the European model of open borders, while we want our borders to be inviolate and secure. They want amnesty for illegals, while we do not. We are committed to ending illegal immigration, and we definitely want Trump to build the wall on the Mexican border.

Of all of the groups who supported Donald Trump, the evangelicals were the largest by far. Eighty-one percent voted for him, which is surprising. I have a difficult time understanding why the percentage was that low. It should have been well over 90 percent.

It isn't that Trump is a paragon of Christian virtue. He isn't, but he does mirror our values, and he's honest about who he is. We liked his transparency and his commitment to appoint conservative justices to the Supreme Court.

Hillary is the exact opposite. It's impossible to enumerate how many times she has been caught lying. Despite this, her deviousness and deceptiveness never seemed to bother the media. This definitely undermined the press' credibility with nearly all of my friends on Facebook.

I believe Hillary would lie, even if the truth would suit her better. It's her default position. Knowing this, I posted about what was really occurring in the election, while it was happening, providing instant rebuttal to Hillary's duplicity.

Regardless of how vicious and caustic Team Clinton became toward Trump, we held firm, knowing what was at stake. We also knew how scheming her surrogates could be. Their malice knew no bounds.

Because I posted about ideas and didn't resort to hateful rhetoric, people responded. By the time the election was held, thousands came to my sight daily for information, wisdom, and hope. They needed assurance that we would prevail. Believing in my cause, I provided consistent affirmations. I did this without hesitation and it was needed, believe me.

Not surprisingly, some Progressives on Facebook opposed me for what I posted. They mocked me for my faith. They scolded me, telling me I had a flawed view of reality. They scoffed at me for maintaining the conviction that we would prevail. To them, we had no reasonable expectation for victory, and they stated that I was misleading my friends by saying there was.

Instead of accepting their prediction about the election's outcome as being accurate, my friends and I rejected their doomful forecast, and we became stronger for doing so. In the process, as things became clearer, our numbers grew and our resolve strengthened.

All we had was each other and the knowledge that our cause was just. In the end, this was all we needed.

I posted routinely. It seemed that there was always something that needed to be addressed. By the 1st of November, I didn't have time to do anything other than respond to those who made comments on my posts. It was exhausting but also exhilarating. I was doing the right thing for the right reason at the right time, and I knew it. Becoming a key player in something as important as saving our nation, which was how nearly all of us viewed it, became very empowering.

While the elites of the mainstream were ecstatic over Hillary's impending victory, congratulating themselves in an intellectual exercise of self-exaltation, I was working relentlessly to make certain her victory never happened. Instead of expostulating platitudes on TV like the mainstream media, I was busy communicating with real human beings on Facebook, and I was doing it one person at a time. In the zero sum game of Presidential politics, I had only one objective. It was to make certain Hillary Clinton never became our next Commander-in-Chief.

My work, as well as a host of others across America, paid off. We were victorious, and Donald J. Trump has become the 45th President of the United States of America.

Since the election, the Left has been scratching their collective heads wondering how we did it. Our feat was so implausible they can't fathom how such an outcome could have happened. They still don't believe it, nor can they accept it. Perhaps they never will.

Although the media was always pessimistic about our chances during the campaign, I remained optimistic. I saw what was happening on the ground. It was much different than what the "talking heads" were discussing on television. I knew a massive voter revolt against the status quo was certain, especially among independents and Christians.

We had had enough of Obama, Hillary, and their politically correct policies. We were ready for a change, and Trump was our guy to bring this about.

That Trump liked us was very important. He sees no reason to apologize for Americans. To him, we are neither deplorable nor irredeemable. That he feels this way is what put us in his corner, and it has kept us solidly entrenched in our support of him.

The Scriptures say that love covers a multitude of sins, and we love Trump. This is the precise reason we have dismissed his numerous faux pas as being insignificant. The Left doesn't take Trump seriously, but they do take his words seriously. We take him very seriously, but we don't necessarily take his words literally—not all of them anyway.

These are some of the specific reasons why we have stood strong for Donald Trump and will continue to do so. Because the Left doesn't understand us, what we believe, or how we think, I decided to write *Creating Trump Nation*. It's not a detailed explanation of what happened during the election. There will be hundreds of idiotic books analyzing that, including some that delve into the impact of Facebook. Like autopsies, these treatises will dissect what happened, providing little else.

Creating Trump Nation is much different. It shows what I actually did, and you can see it for yourself. It's a "Real Time" look at what happened during the campaign, precisely when it was occurring. For privacy reasons, I have not added the responses, but they are all still on my Facebook page—thousands of them.

Picking up at the campaign at the end of February, there are numerous substantive posts about the election. Each was written and posted in the heat of battle. The posts were how I interpreted events, while they were occurring. They show what deplorable people like me thought about events. By reading the entries, you can see for yourself what influenced us. You will come to understand why we grew stronger in our resolve, producing a commitment that became unshakable. Although occasionally rattled, we hung in there and became victorious.

Now that triumph has been achieved, the only thing we want is for President Trump to do what he promised he would do. That's all. He said he would never let us down, and we believe him. We are counting on him—all of us. Like him, we want to make America great again.

For those of you on the Left who are appalled by what we have accomplished, I have no intention of rubbing our victory in your face. That would be unseemly, but I do believe you can learn a great deal from the posts I have written. Reading them will enlighten you and give you keen insight into why deplorables like me reject your godless Progressive worldview.

You don't understand us because you refuse to pay attention. You don't listen to us. You never have. Even worse, you don't believe we have anything worthwhile to say. Instead, you talk among yourselves, dismissing us as being unimportant. Reading my posts will provide you with an idea about what we believe and what motivates us to action. If you want to win elections anyplace other than the West Coast and the Northeast, you need to pay attention to what we believe. If possible, you need to take our beliefs to heart.

The reason my site became so popular is because I have the capacity to articulate what evangelicals and patriotic Americans believe in words that resonate. For those of you who identify with this category, reading *Creating Trump Nation* will help you fortify and solidify your belief system. It will also be a soul satisfying exercise.

My posts are chronological and presented just as I wrote them during the campaign. Like many others, I started out supporting another candidate. I was for Cruz until I saw the crowd Trump had in Bethpage, New York, right after Cruz's "reset" win in Wisconsin. That's when I realized Cruz had no chance of winning up North. He couldn't even compete. Because defeating Hillary was more important than anything else, I started to support Trump and never looked back.

I position my posts as being COMMON SENSE for two reasons. First, what I wrote is common sense, at least for patriots. Second, it is a historical reference to Thomas Paine's writings that justified the American Revolution.

I haven't changed my posts in any way. The only thing I have added is a headline to provide a contextual statement. I have also added the Real Clear Politics average for each day, just to show you the size of the mountain we were required to climb. We were always behind.

By reading each post from hindsight, like a Monday morning quarterback, you will see how my positions evolved. Clearly, I was misinformed about several things, but that's what makes *Creating Trump Nation* so important. Not everything was clear, especially in the heat of the battle. Coming to the truth, like it should be, was a constant struggle of iron sharpening iron, as my readers and I went back and forth. In the end, it was a worthwhile effort.

For those in politics, if you want to gain insight, *Creating Trump Nation* is actually a "How To Manual" to get elected in the future. The old way, Hillary's way, is expensive and it will never work again. To her legion of sycophantic media followers, I will be perceived as a marginal player at best, but such a perception is a mistake.

In the body politic, along with numerous others, I have become the new Leviathan. To those who are discerning, you'll recognize that I am the voice of the future—not of the past. The days of achieving victory by spending billions on TV ads has become as irrelevant as a Ghetto Blaster.

The era of issue oriented, micro targeting through the Internet has arrived. Because we utilized Facebook effectively, we have taken back our nation. We intend to make America great again, and we will never again bow our collective knees to the godless Progressives. The era of Political Correctness is over, thanks to Trump. We will never allow the views espoused by Hillary Clinton, Barack Obama, or any other near-do-well waiting in the wings to ever enslave our minds again. That is our unshakable resolve.

One last thing: Even if we had lost, nothing about what I have written would have changed, nor would my commitment to the principles I espouse. They will never change.

—Jack Watts

The 2016
Presidential Campaign on
Facebook

We Are Taking Back Our Nation

Real Clear Politics Average
RCP: Clinton – 45.3 Trump – 42.5

COMMON SENSE: At this time in 1980, when I was in my Ph.D. program at Emory University studying International Politics, all of my professors and fellow graduate students believed the United States was in irreversible decline. Our economy was stagnant; Iran was making a fool out of us by holding our Embassy staff hostage; and we were being led by an incompetent President— Jimmy Carter. In other words, the situation then mirrors today's situation quite well.

The Republican Presidential aspirants were bickering, and nobody thought a true conservative like Ronald Reagan, who was consistently described as a "Right-Wing Extremist," could win the election. It was the opinion of the intellectual elite, in both the press and academia, that to nominate Reagan would hand the election to Carter, which is exactly what they wanted. After all, according to them, Carter had a more realistic viewpoint about America's prospects for the future. Again, the situation then was a mirror of what we are being told by the intellectuals and Left-Wing media today. They do not believe a true conservative can win the White House, or more accurately, they don't want one to be victorious.

They were wrong then—just as they are wrong now. Reagan

was a principled Conservative—a man who ushered in an unprecedented era of prosperity as well as victory in the Cold War. Today, we have at least two candidates capable of doing similar things. Do not believe those who say this isn't possible.

Just as in 1980, when the American people had had enough of incompetence, whining defeatism, and an entitlement mindset, Americans today are fed up with global retreat, a weakened military, corruption, mind-numbing waste, and the idea that America is in irreversible economic decline.

We have been a great nation and can be once again—but certainly not under the leadership of Hillary Clinton or The Bern. So, gird your minds for the battle that lies ahead, as we bow our collective knees to Almighty God and take back the country we love, restoring the values of our forefathers—none of whom were Progressives or Muslims.

2/28

Trump is Making Some Smart Moves
RCP: Clinton – 45.3 Trump – 42.5

COMMON SENSE: As a Trump nomination seems increasingly likely, rumors swirl about him naming Newt Gingrich Chief of Staff and Chris Christie to a key cabinet position, perhaps Attorney General. If this is the direction he is headed, getting behind his nomination—if it happens—will be much easier. Having been Speaker of the House and the chief architect for our last balanced budget, Newt would really help get things done. As a prosecutor, Christie's credentials are solid, and he is fearless.

By letting us know who he would tap for key positions—like a Parliamentarian model—much of the fear behind a Trump Presidency would dissipate, at least for Conservatives. It's a smart move on his part, and I hope he continues with it.

Obama's Failed Economy

RCP: Clinton – 45.3 Trump – 42.5

COMMON SENSE: The United States has now gone a record 10 straight years without 3 percent growth in real Gross Domestic Product. Since the 1930s, there is only one ten-year stretch—2006 through 2015—when the annual growth in real GDP never hit 3 percent. By any standard, this period, which includes the entire time of Obama's Presidency, has been a pitiful performance.

During the last ten years, real annual growth in GDP peaked in 2006 at 2.7 percent. It has never been that high again. The reason why is simple: President Obama's focus has been upon dismantling America's means of production, rather than growing it. Under Obama's leadership, there has been virtually no growth, and Hillary Clinton will do no better. Currently, 94 million people are out of the workforce, the largest number since Jimmy Carter's failed leadership.

We are currently $19 trillion in debt, which equates to $159,294 per taxpayer. This is up more than $100,000 since Obama took office, which begs the question: Are you $100,000 better off than when he took office? If not, you might want to vote for your own economic best interest, rather than for continuing to squander the wealth America has accumulated for generations.

Change is in order. With 46 million in poverty and 45 million on Food Stamps, we simply cannot afford four more years of Obama's failed policies. Hillary Clinton would be nothing more than Obama 3.0. So, unless you are a fool or on the dole, vote for someone who has the capacity to generate growth and restore prosperity to the United States of America.

3/1

Republican Foolishness May Hand Hillary the Election

RCP: Clinton – 46.5 Trump – 43.5

COMMON SENSE: I don't care about the size of Trump's hands, Rubio's ears, or Cruz's nose. What does concern me is focusing on such trivial nonsense may disaffect so many voters that Hillary Clinton, who is the epitome of deceitfulness and corruption, may become our next President.

Now that all of her deleted emails have been retrieved, we know that she lied about their content. More than 2,000 contained classified material, which she knew or should have known, was a significant security breach. We simply cannot allow someone who is this unethical to become our next Commander-in-Chief. Her failure to do her duty reveals a pattern of behavior that is criminal. If Loretta Lynch, Obama's Attorney General, brings Hillary's conduct to a Grand Jury, the former Secretary of State will be indicted, as she should be.

The damage Hillary has done foreshadows how she would behave as President, and it is unacceptable. Therefore, I implore the Republican candidates to abandon their foolish body comparisons and focus on what is vital to our national interest—defeating Hillary Clinton.

3/3

Hillary's Email Scandal Intensifies
RCP: Clinton – 45.4 Trump – 42.0

COMMON SENSE: The case against Hillary Clinton, for using an unsecured server for classified emails, is moving along well. By giving Brian Pagliano—the IT tech who installed the server—immunity from prosecution, we know that a secret Grand Jury has already heard evidence against Hillary and her subordinates. This had to occur. It's the only way for a federal judge to have granted immunity. Neither the FBI nor the Department of Justice has the power to do this—only a judge.

Obviously, there is compelling evidence against the former Secretary of state, and it's all going to come out, perhaps very soon. When it does, there will be indictments, probably against Umma Abadeen and Cheryl Mills, perhaps even Hillary.

By giving Pagliano immunity, he will be forced to provide full disclosure. If he doesn't, his immunity from prosecution will be revoked. This is very bad news for Hillary because the government now has an inside witness—someone who knows exactly what happened and who was responsible for everything.

With Hillary about to sew up the nomination, the timing of this couldn't be worse for the Democrats. If she is forced out, her supporters will be angry. If Joe Biden or John Kerry tried to take her place, Bernie Sanders' supporters will cry foul. This should be great news for the Republicans, who might consider dwelling on something other than big ears and small hands. Otherwise, they will snatch defeat from the jaws of victory—just like they did with the Romney and McCain campaigns.

One more thing: This dispels the false narrative of Team Hillary that the FBI investigation concerns a "Security Review." Nonsense! Immunity is only granted in major criminal investigations, which is exactly what this is, despite what Hillary is telling the fawning media and her gullible supporters.

3/3

Mitt's Rebuke Will Not Hurt Trump
RCP: Clinton – 45.4 Trump – 42.0

COMMON SENSE: I am for Ted Cruz. I've been very clear about this. Nevertheless, I am deeply offended by the way the Republican Establishment is trying to undermine the candidacy of Donald Trump. It is my hope that Cruz will prevail, but if he doesn't and Trump wins the nomination, I will support Trump enthusiastically. The alternative, Hillary Clinton, would be worse than another four years of He-Who-Must-Not-Be-Blamed.

Mitt Romney calling Trump a con and a fraud is untrue and ridiculous. It also says that we, the American people, are too stupid to know what's best for us, which is really galling. Since we've had a steady diet of condescension from Obama for two terms, it isn't something we are willing to have shoved down our throats again. If Romney had been as forceful about Obama in 2012, instead of weak and vacillating, he might have won the election.

One more thing: Rubio's attempts to insult Trump reminds me of a twelve-year-old trying to swear, but not knowing how to string the words together properly.

3/4

NOTE TO RINO'S:
We Are Tired of Your Falures
RCP: Clinton – 45.4 Trump – 42.0

COMMON SENSE: For a long time, I considered Marco Rubio to be a suitable candidate, but I have become extremely tired of his incessant badgering. The only people who think he has a chance are career Republicans like Romney, who has done little more than make a fool of himself.

When a baseball team is underachieving, you fire the manager not the players. It's the same in politics. Collectively, we are firing our RINO leaders, and they can't stand it. Evidently, they prefer losing elections, rather than making bold new changes. This is why they hate Trump and Cruz—both of whom refuse to play by the establishment rules.

It's a new day. Energy and momentum are on our side, and we will not be stopped. We are taking back our nation.

3/17

Because I am an Adult, I Will Vote for Trump

RCP: Clinton – 48.2 Trump – 40.2

COMMON SENSE: In an intense Presidential election cycle, it's important to differentiate between what is important and what is less than important. If you don't, you will be captivated by all sorts of trivial things that will throw you into a meaningless frenzy. Here are some things that are important:

1. We are over $19 trillion in debt—half of it from Obama. Who can change the dynamics so that we will once again be prosperous?

2. Our standing in the world has diminished. Our friends don't

trust us, and our enemies don't fear us. Who has the capacity to strengthen the military and be an effective Commander-in-Chief?

3. Millions of Radical Islamic Jihadists believe the USA is the Great Satan and want to behead us. Who is strong enough to identify the problem accurately, confront it head-on, and destroy this threat?

4. Our Southern border is a joke. More illegals are coming through this year than ever before. Who will change this?

5. Our healthcare system, once the envy of the world, has been purposefully destroyed. Who can fix it?

6. Currently, 93 million people are out of the workforce. Who can create jobs and not just talk about it?

These are important questions. The following issues are not:

1. Who has the biggest ears, smallest hands, etc?

2. Who has ties to Goldman-Sachs?

3. Whose wife would make the best First Lady?

4. Who do the polls say has the best chance of beating Hillary?

5. Another 1,000 idiotic questions like these.

Keep your eye on the ball, y'all, and everything else will work out. Hillary is vulnerable. The only way she can win is if we continue to self-destruct. This is why I write COMMON SENSE. My hope is that people will use common sense, rather than get caught up in meaningless minutia.

3/19

A Vote for Hillary is a Vote for Global Retreat

RCP: Clinton – 48.5 Trump – 39.8

COMMON SENSE: Remember when Iran detained sailors from the US Navy earlier this year? When this happened, what was the response of the Obama administration? Secretary of State John Kerry thanked Iran for treating our sailors so well. No kidding.

Is this the kind of leadership we want? Is this the kind of leadership we deserve?

Being the cause of all the problems in the world, according to Progressives like Hillary and The Bern, such treatment is what we deserve. Do you agree with them? I certainly don't.

Because of Obama's flawed worldview, implemented by Hillary and John Kerry, America is now in full retreat globally, which has destabilized the Middle East, Eastern Europe, and even Latin America.

If this is what you want, Hillary is your girl. If it isn't, then stop fretting and get behind either Cruz or Trump—both of whom are committed to restoring the military to pre-Obama effectiveness.

3/20

A "No" for Trump is a "Yes" for Hillary
RCP: Clinton – 48.5 Trump – 39.8

COMMON SENSE: Let me try and help you understand something that is very important. Politics is a Zero Sum Game. This means one person wins an election, while the other person loses it. There is no middle ground, no silver metal for second place, and no consolation prize. It's winner take all.

This is not only true for the candidates, but it is also true for the electorate. Let me explain.

In November, there will be two viable choices for President. Most likely, the choices will be Donald Trump and Hillary Clinton. You can vote for either one or the other, but there is no middle ground between the two. Abstaining from voting, based on antipathy toward either one, is still a vote in this Zero Sum Game. Not voting for one aids the other.

Not voting for Trump because of his many real or perceived flaws aids Clinton—period. To believe that not participating has some redeemable value is nonsense—not in a Zero Sum Game. If politics wasn't a Zero Sum Game, taking such a position would be fine, perhaps even noble, but since it is winner take all, it isn't. It's foolhardy—the position of a petulant child.

This is just as true for idealists on the Left as it is for Conservatives on the Right. For a millennial, who idealistically supports Sanders, to refuse to vote for Hillary, just because she's a criminal, is tacit support for Trump. Every non-vote for her is a vote for Trump.

For supporters of other Republican candidates to sit out the election, refusing to vote for Trump, would provide support for Hillary. Each non-vote for him is a vote for her. Since her policies, character, and integrity are so egregious, in good conscience, I have no choice, other than to vote for Donald Trump. It's the role I must play in this Zero Sum Game. I have to; it's my responsibility as a citizen.

We Must Stop Hillary from Becoming Commander-in-Chief

RCP: Clinton – 49.0 Trump – 39.2

COMMON SENSE: Soon, the FBI will conclude its investigation of Hillary Clinton. When they do, they will ask that their findings be presented to a grand jury for indictment.

When this happens, President Obama may pardon Hillary, which he has the Constitutional authority to do, even before she is indicted. This will infuriate Conservatives but not Progressives. Hillary will not lose much support from her base. They do not care that she is a corrupt, duplicitous criminal. They will vote for her anyway because she supports give-away programs and legitimizing depravity. They recognize what is in their best interest.

On the other side, there are more than enough hard-working, God-fearing people to prevent Hillary from becoming our next President, but she will probably win the office anyway. That's because millions of Christians are too noble, too pure, and too self-important to get their hands dirty in the messy business of voting for a candidate who is flawed.

The Democrats do it all the time. They have no problem voting for a criminal like Hillary, but Republicans seem to be incapable of uniting around anybody who has even the slightest flaw; and our next nominee has quite a few.

Instead of uniting to stop the common Evil, believers by the millions will wring their hands in despair, bemoaning the future of the nation, begging God to spare them, while they have it within their power to stop someone like Hillary dead in her tracks. They just won't do it.

This year, the stakes are higher than ever. While Secretary of State, Hillary was responsible for selling American uranium to Russia, who in turn sold it to Iran. Now, the Iranians are busy building nukes—thanks to Obama and John Kerry—intended for Tel Aviv and New York.

If Christians unite, Hillary can be stopped. We still have time to prevent our own destruction, but it will require the united efforts of all good men and women—not just a fraction of us.

Being passive in the face of Evil is to embrace it. It's time to take our nation back from leaders who are not patriots. Be strong, be brave, and be willing to get your hands dirty for the greater good. Do it for your children, your grandchildren, and for those who have died to keep us free.

3/22

Why so Many Christians Abstain from Voting

RCP: Clinton – 49.0 Trump – 39.2

COMMON SENSE: From our earliest settlers—the Pilgrims and the Puritans—we have had two simultaneous traditions present in American society. The Pilgrims wanted nothing to do with the world, especially politics, believing that it was morally wrong to get involved. "Why polish brass on a sinking ship," was what they believed.

The Puritans were the exact opposite. They wanted to fix what was wrong and worked diligently to create a model for the Motherland, England, to emulate.

Not surprisingly, the Puritans and Pilgrims did not get along. Eventually, the Pilgrims were driven out. They traveled south. Led by Roger Williams, they established Providence and created their own university to teach the "true religion"—Brown University. The Puritans remained in Boston, establishing Harvard, followed by Yale a few years later.

Throughout the centuries, both traditions have been present. The separatist tradition has been strongest among the independent Baptist churches—not to be confused with the Southern Baptists. Traditionally, Separatist Baptists have refrained from getting involved with politics, which they consider beneath them. They

rarely voted until 1980, when Jerry Falwell led the movement—
The Moral Majority—to get them involved, and he was quite successful.

Nevertheless, the natural inclination of believers like these is to
refrain from getting "involved with the world." So, it should be no
surprise that millions of God-fearing people refuse to do what
those of us from the Puritan tradition believe is our God-mandat-
ed responsibility—voting in elections. We view their position as
ridiculous, saying they are so spiritually minded that they are no
earthly good, while they view us as stained by the world. It's been
this way since the 1620s, and it's not about to change. So, my
advice is to be patient with people who disagree with you because
you can't change them.

3/22

Progressives, By Nature, Cannot Defeat Islamic Terrorism

RCP: Clinton – 49.0 Trump – 39.2

COMMON SENSE: Concerning terrorism, there is a fundamental
difference between the way the Left sees it and how the Right
does. Progressives—like Obama, Hillary, Kerry, and The Bern—
believe we have caused Islamic people to hate us, which makes
the lion's share of the problem ours. So, what we need to do is
make the lives of Radical Jihadists better. If we do, in time, the

problem will solve itself. Be nice to them and they will eventually be nice to us. Besides, there are only a few who have been radicalized. The rest of Islam is peaceful.

Conservatives—like Trump, Cruz, Netanyahu, and others—believe that the problem originates with the way Islam views the world. Those who take the Koran literally—the Radical Jihadists—believe the USA is filled with infidels, making us the Great Satan. Therefore, by nature we are Evil and deserve to be the object of terror. Jews are even worse than us and need to be exterminated.

Conservatives believe the problem originates with the belief system of Muslims. Therefore, for a Conservative to make policies based on being nice to Jihadists would be viewed as cowardly, capitulating to Evil. The way to defeat Islamic terrorism is to identify it, call it what it is, and make policies aimed at defeating them militarily, sending them back to the Stone Age.

In this upcoming election, the choice Americans make will go a long way toward either solving the problem or making it worse. If you believe Muslims hate us for good reason, vote for Hillary or The Bern. They will govern in a similar way to Obama, which is to not deal with the problem effectively. If you think Radical Islam is Evil and needs to be defeated decisively, vote for Trump or Cruz. They will not coddle terrorists, and they recognize there is a fundamental problem with the belief system of Muslims.

The media and our feckless national leaders want to make this issue more complex than it is. It's as simple as what I have just described. There's a reason why they want to keep you confused.

If we accept their version of reality as accurate, we will continue to be more passive than aggressive in confronting the problem, and that's what they want. After all, America is responsible for causing all of the problems in the world. Everybody, other than Conservatives, realizes that.

3/23

No Progressive Can Win Against ISIS

RCP: Clinton – 50.4 Trump – 39.0

COMMON SENSE: Despite the dramatic upsurge in power by ISIS, resulting in worldwide carnage, the Obama administration fully intends to empty GITMO—just to fulfill a campaign pledge to Hollywood's radical Left. This is not only foolhardy, but it also provides a clue as to why no Progressive can adequately lead the fight against global terrorism. Let me explain why.

Progressives—like Obama, Hillary, Kerry, and The Bern—do not see the world as it really is. They see it through the prism of their flawed ideology. Because Progressives are non-theistic, even if they maintain rudimentary god-consciousness, they cannot fathom how Islamic Jihadists think, which is in chiliastic terms. Radical Muslims believe in their 12th Caliphate as strongly as evangelicals believe in the Second Coming of Christ. Because the Progressive worldview is materialistic and not spiritual, they can't understand those who have an entirely different perspective.

Consequently, the only answers Progressives have for the problems are based on what they know. Progressives believe Muslim unrest is caused by poverty and hopelessness. It's also because of global warming. Muslims don't want to live in the hot desert. It's because their population is exploding, and they need more room to grow and expand. They need to know we want to help them.

None of these answers are accurate. They have nothing to do with global Jihadism. Muslims are terrorists because it's what Allah has commanded them to be—plain and simple. They are afraid of hell more than they are afraid of death, and your mortal enemies are Israel and the Great Satan—the USA.

If your worldview is Judeo-Christian, you may not like the Islamic perspective but you can understand it. If you are a Progressive, you cannot. For a Progressive, it simply doesn't compute. Unfortunately, we are being led by Progressives who are incapable of understanding this seminal problem. Thus, they are incapable of defending us adequately against Radical Islam.

Hillary has proven she doesn't have a clue about what motivates Muslims. As Secretary of State, she was a disaster. If she becomes Commander-in-Chief, ISIS will continue to grow, despite the Leftist rhetoric that consistently denies that it will. To defeat ISIS, you not only have to identify it correctly, but you also have to understand what motivates it to be convinced that wanton terrorism is a good thing. Why so few understand how simple this concept is beyond me, but they don't.

3/24

Obama, the American Nero

RCP: Clinton – 50.0 Trump – 38.8

COMMON SENSE: President Obama doing the wave at a baseball game, sitting beside a ruthless dictator, conjures images of Nero fiddling while Rome burned. This isn't the first time Obama has been in the wrong place at the wrong time, when terrorism has reared its ugly head, nor is it the worst. Playing golf ten minutes after speaking about Foley's decapitation may have been more inappropriate, or perhaps Obama partying with Beyonce in Vegas the night after the Benghazi attack was.

Such images of Obama being asleep at the wheel tell us a great deal about the man. If these attacks had been perpetrated upon Muslims by Christians or Jews, do you believe Obama would be so cavalier about them? I do not. His outrage would be palpable.

The reason Obama doesn't take these assaults and others like them seriously is they do not fit into his narrative of reality. Consequently, he denies the gravity of what is happening by doing what he does best, having fun. At this point in his administration, being a lame duck, he is more disengaged than ever, choosing to double-down on his core beliefs that Islam is a religion of Peace and there is no reason to keep GITMO open. After all, we have won the War on Terror—at least according to America's version of Nero.

3/25

Hillary's FBI Crisis Looms Above Every Other Issue

RCP: Clinton – 50.0 Trump – 39.8

COMMON SENSE: Make no mistake about it—the most important issue of the 2016 Presidential Election is still out there. No, it's not the War on Terror, unsustainable debt, or securing the border from illegal immigration. It concerns the Rule of Law. Will we be a nation where nobody is above the law, which has always been our tradition, or will some people be treated differently, remaining above the law?

Currently, there are 150 FBI agents investigating Hillary Clinton's unethical, corrupt, and illegal activities, while she served as Secretary of State. When they present their findings to Loretta Lynch, Obama's Attorney General, and ask her to present them to a grand jury, the moment of truth will arrive.

At that point, the issue will become a political question. This is when President Obama will either rise to the occasion and do the right thing, or when he will refuse to abide by the Constitution and will not allow the FBI's findings to move forward.

At that precise moment, we will know where we are as a nation. Does the Rule of Law still apply to everyone or doesn't it? Millions cynically believe Obama will disregard his Constitutional responsibilities, while millions more are so obtuse about what is happening, they will be clueless about the seriousness of the matter.

I hope Obama directs Loretta Lynch to allow the legal system to move forward unimpeded. He should just stay out of it all together, but I have serious doubts that he could do that. If he refuses to allow justice to take its course, we will have a Constitutional crisis as serious as during the Watergate scandal. Perhaps Obama knows this and doesn't want his legacy to be stained by such dishonor. Perhaps he doesn't care. Only time will tell. Until that moment arrives, we will all remain in limbo about the defining issue in the next election.

3/31

Hillary's Candidacy Is Weak, Very Weak

RCP: Clinton – 49.7 Trump – 39.1

COMMON SENSE: Amazingly, people seem to think Hillary Clinton's election to the White House is inevitable, when the exact opposite is true. In reality, she is the weakest candidate running . . . by far.

Let me explain. In states that normally vote for a Democrat in the general election, she is being trounced by The Bern—a clueless Socialist, but also a decent man. When I say trounced, I mean decimated. In last week's primaries, for example, The Bern received more than 70 percent of the vote.

Where Hillary is supposed to be strong, as the Democratic nominee, she is weak, but she does have a sizable lead in the delegates. The reason for this, other than the corruptible Super Delegates, is Hillary has been soundly defeated by The Bern in many states. Being first, SC was Hillary's "Firewall," according to the pundits. She beat The Bern handily, but in a General Election, what do you think Hillary's chances are of winning SC? Let me tell you: Zero!

Regardless of who the Republicans choose their candidate will beat Hillary in South Carolina. The same is true in every other Southern state where Hillary won in the Democratic Primary. In the General Election, she will not win any of these states, but none of the commentators ever mention this, do they?

In the states she needs to win—the Blue States—she is losing big time, and in the states she has no chance of taking from the Republicans—the Red States—she seems strong, but it's only because of the black community, which isn't large enough to carry any Southern State. This alone shows you exactly how vulnerable she is, especially if the Republicans ever get their act together, which they may not.

One more thing: We still have not heard what the FBI has to say about her criminal behavior. When we do, the few people who mistakenly believe she is trustworthy and honest may change their minds.

4/2

Inept Obama Lectures Trump on Foreign Policy

RCP: Clinton – 49.7 Trump – 39.1

COMMON SENSE: President Obama, sporting a contemptuous, condescending sneer, lectured Donald Trump about foreign policy yesterday. After all, foreign policy is our Nobel-Peace-Prize-winning President's strong suit, isn't it?

It should be, but it isn't. Despite the predictable fawning adulation of the media, those who desperately try to spin reality to make Obama look good, his foreign policy has been such a colossal failure that he actually makes Jimmy Carter's record of ineptitude look good.

For example:

—Along with his toady, Hillary Clinton, Obama hit the "Reset Button" with Russia, but he never saw Russia's annex of the Crimea or invasion of Ukraine coming, did he? Of course he didn't. Yet, he mocked Mitt Romney—just like he did Trump—for even suggesting Russia might be contemplating aggression. In Eastern Europe, Obama has been clueless.

—Obama backed the Muslim Brotherhood in Egypt, calling them reformers. What was the end result of this mistake? Obama destabilized Egypt—a strong and dependable ally of America for the past forty years.

—Obama, along with Hillary Clinton, undermined Muammar Gaddafi, destabilizing Libya. This ended with the massacre in Benghazi, which our profound Commander-in-Chief blamed on a

You Tube video clip—all to ensure his reelection.

—Obama told us that he has won the war on terror, and ISIS was nothing more than a JV team, which it certainly is not.

—Obama drew a "Red Line" with Syria, concerning chemical warfare, which he refused to back up, letting our enemies know how weak and spineless he is.

—Obama, along with John Kerry, negotiated a deal with Iran over nuclear weapons that will allow the world's leading sponsor of terror to obtain nukes with impunity. Of all of his failures, this is the most egregious, and may lead to World War III or Armageddon.

Obama's failures are astounding. Yet, he has the audacity to lecture Trump and others. As a result on Obama's failed leadership, our enemies do not fear us, and our allies do not trust us. While Brussels burned, Obama danced the Tango, which he couldn't do right either.

Stealing Delegates from Trump Shoould Not Be Allowed

RCP: Clinton – 49.7 Trump – 39.1

COMMON SENSE: In America, we do not have a more highly valued belief than abiding by the will of the people, when they vote. I certainly do not like President Obama's policies or beliefs, but he won the election. So, he is my President. This makes me the loyal opposition. The operative word is loyal. That's how we operate in America.

In the Georgia primary, I voted for Cruz, but Trump won the state easily—just like he won Tennessee and Louisiana. He won these states fair and square. Yet, in Tennessee and Louisiana, the Republican establishment is trying to take his delegates away from him. That's not right; it's not American; and it's as sleazy as something Bill and Hillary Clinton would do.

I am offended that the Republican establishment is unwilling to abide by this basic core value. The will of the people is for Trump, so he deserves all of the delegates he has earned. There is no right way to do a wrong thing. Depriving Trump of his due is unethical, and voters like me, who did not vote for him, will not stand for it.

EDIT: It's the ethicality of disenfranchising the voters that offends me. It offends me for Bernie Sanders too. In the case of the Democrats, at least they are doing it up-front—not behind closed doors.

Kasich! Get Out Now

RCP: Clinton – 49.4 Trump – 38.6

COMMON SENSE: Why is John Kasich still in the race? Why is he still receiving as much attention as Donald Trump and Ted Cruz? Kasich has no chance of winning the nomination—not one in a million. Yet, he is still out there peddling his ideas—like he's a viable candidate—and the media treats him like he's still in the running.

He just doesn't have enough integrity to bow out gracefully, that's all. Bush, Rubio, Walker, and even Lindsey Graham had enough integrity to do so, but not Kasich.

If I were Trump or Cruz, I would demand that Kasich not be included in any debates or anything else. All Kasich wants to do is deny Trump the nomination and create a brokered convention—something the voters do not want. If anybody thinks Kasich is helping Cruz think again. He isn't. Kasich's sleazy attempts to nullify the will of the voters should make all of us look at him like he has you-know-what on the soles of his shoes. That doesn't smell very good, and neither does he.

Kasich, you have no following and should get out of the race—NOW!

Was Bernie Right About Hillary or Not?

RCP: Clinton – 47.4 Trump – 38.4

COMMON SENSE: Bernie Sanders is wrong. Hillary Clinton is definitely qualified to be President of the United States. It isn't that she is unqualified; it's that she is unfit to serve. Pathologically deceitful and corrupt to the bone, she is untrustworthy at every level.

Because the fawning media has made Americans believe Hillary's Presidency is inevitable, millions live in despair, believing we are doomed, but nothing could be further from the truth. She can't even put away a seventy-four-year-old Socialist, who isn't even a Democrat.

Wait until she is nominated and her duplicity is revealed to the American people in one attack ad after the other. Americans may not understand the nuances of deception involved in selling our uranium to the Russians, but everybody will understand that, when she was First Lady, she stole $193,000 worth of dishes and silverware from the White House, when her husband's Presidency was over. Even Neanderthals will know that was theft—pure and simple. She didn't rectify it until last year, just before announcing her candidacy. One more thing; we still don't know what the FBI has discovered . . . but we will.

4/8

What's Behind the Trump Phenomenon?

RCP: Clinton – 49.0 Trump – 39.2

COMMON SENSE: Many have tried to explain the Trump phenomenon, but most are clueless. To begin with, you must understand the mindset of the American people. It isn't anger and hatred they feel, as much as it is righteous indignation. There's a difference—a big difference.

Trump has tapped into this. Call it the American spirit that demands righteousness, regardless of how it is achieved. It's the "Frontier Thesis" of Frederick Jackson Turner for a new millennium. People who like Trump are not racists and bigots, as the liberal media would have you believe. His supporters are rugged individualists who demand not only personal freedom but also personal accountability.

For people like these, and there are millions of them, Trump is as heroic as John Wayne, with the snarly edge of Dirty Harry. His supporters loathe the sappy weakness of Progressives, every bit as much as they champion American exceptionalism. Trumpsters, because of the strength of their convictions, will not back down when trouble arises. Instead, like Dirty Harry, they will head toward it.

How many rugged individualists are there in America, as compared to those who want something for nothing, I'm uncertain, but I do suspect there are enough to give Trump the Republican nomination on the 1st ballot. Even if Trump goes down to ignominious defeat, he has stirred something in the American consciousness—like Barry Goldwater did in 1964—and a new wave of patriotic strength is certain to emerge from it.

4/10

The Iranian Nuke Deal Ensures World War III

RCP: Clinton – 50.4 Trump – 39.0

COMMON SENSE: Let me be perfectly clear about this: ObamaCare is good policy, when compared to the disastrous deal the Obama Administration made, concerning the Iranian nuke deal. Our negotiator, John Kerry, was taken to the cleaners by the Ayatollahs. The Iranian nuke program—now free from inspection—is racing forward, fully intent on ushering in the 12th Caliphate. From an American perspective, that's World War III. From a millennial perspective, it's Armageddon. Regardless of how you cut it, this ill-suited deal may cost millions of lives, which is exactly what Iran wants, even if it means their own annihilation.

Even though Obama and Kerry are fully aware that they have been had, they cannot put Humpty Dumpty back together again. Their legacy will be forever tarnished—just like Neville Chamberlain's. Even worse, grade schoolers in America will pay for this mistake with their lives—no question about it.

4/11

The Delegate Fiasco

RCP: Clinton – 49.6 Trump – 39.0

COMMON SENSE: Donald Trump isn't a stupid man, but it looks like he doesn't understand the rules of the game he is playing. Because he doesn't have the organization that Cruz has, Trump is crying foul, making people believe he is being cheated. On the surface, it appears that he is.

Because the system favors the establishment, at the expense of individual voters, Trump is making his case to the American people. It's a brilliant idea, and I think it's going to work. Trump is making Cruz look sleazy for simply following the rules. Trump's outrage is aimed at New York, Pennsylvania, New Jersey, and California voters—not the uncommitted delegates Cruz is putting in his back pocket from Colorado and other states.

To think that Trump doesn't know what he is doing is naive. He knows exactly what he is doing. His strategy, which marginalizes Cruz, will ensure that the turnout for future elections favors him, and the delegates from those contests go into the Trump column.

4/12

The Cruz/Trump Fiasco Is Self-Defeating

RCP: Clinton – 49.0 Trump – 39.2

COMMON SENSE: At my fraternity, Kappa Sigma, each year we held a "Pig Party." On that evening, each brother would ask out a really ugly girl, bring her over to the fraternity house, and we would laugh at all of them behind their backs, secretly choosing the Queen. Although I never participated, I was a brother, so these were the kind of guys I associated with. Many fraternities did things like this—not just ours.

The brothers loved to mock these girls, who had no idea how badly they were being ridiculed. It was a terrible thing to do, but it illustrates an important point. In my analogy, Ted Cruz is the Ugly Girl who is being courted by the Republican Establishment.

Cruz is all smiles, believing he actually has gained the support of Washington D.C., RINOs, but he hasn't. They are using him, mocking him behind his back, just waiting for the opportunity to humiliate him, dropping him like a hot potato. Sadly, like the unfortunate girls, who believed a handsome guy saw through the veneer of unattractiveness to their inner beauty, Cruz believes the Republican Establishment is embracing his candidacy. Just like the Pig Party, everything about it is deceptive.

Rather than bask in the false glow of this scam, Cruz would be much better served to make peace with Donald Trump, and viase-versa. If the two men unite, which would require wisdom and discernment from both of them—a tall order—the RINOs would not be strong enough to accomplish their goal, which is to snatch the nomination away from both of them.

The only way for the Establishment to achieve its goal, which is to nominate Kasich or someone else, is for the Cruz and Trump to remain enmeshed in their adolescent squabbles. So far, just like my fraternity brothers, this nefarious RINO strategy is working, and they are laughing—just like the Kappa Sigs did at the ugly girls so many years ago.

4/14

The "Fix" Is Set for Hillary

RCP: Clinton – 49.0 Trump – 39.1

COMMON SENSE: This may be the most direct and clearly stated announcement President Obama has ever made. It should give all of us comfort, knowing that Hillary Clinton's criminal activity will finally be addressed—just like it would be for any other American. The Rule of Law will be followed; justice will prevail; and Hillary will be indicted.

Despite Obama's unambiguous clarity, I don't believe what he said for one minute; do you? After seven years of repeated deception, to accept Obama's promise at face value would be as foolhardy as taking an alcoholic's promise that he will never drink again. In fact, the more he guarantees the process will be honest, the more certain I am that the fix is in place.

Don't Be Afraid of the Polls, Not Yet

RCP: Clinton – 49.0   Trump – 39.1

COMMON SENSE: I need to address something most people don't understand. Both Bernie and John Kasich poll well because they have not been relentlessly attacked like Cruz and Trump, especially Trump. Even Hillary has remained virtually untouched—so far at least.

Because neither The Bern nor Kasich have the slightest chance of being nominated, they have remained free from attack ads. At the same time, because so many fear a Trump Presidency, he has received millions of dollars worth of attack ads. Naturally, his favorables have gone down, while those who are not attacked tend to rise.

In a general election, all of this will change, however, and it will change fast—especially when the Super PACs go after Hillary's incompetence and corruption. So, don't let the media influence you into abandoning your candidate. Remain strong and let the chips fall where they may.

4/20

Trump Is Cleary the Choice of the People

RCP: Clinton – 48.8 Trump – 39.5

COMMON SENSE: What a blowout in Bethpage, New York, for Donald Trump. When the primaries began, I liked Walker, Rubio, and Cruz, eventually landing on Cruz. I liked him because of his commitment to the Constitution and the Rule of Law, which President Obama has never followed or honored. Of the seventeen candidates, like so many others, I considered the Trump candidacy to be a joke, but I was wrong.

He is clearly he choice of the people, despite what the Republican establishment wants. Since the RINOs have given us McCain and Romney—both of whom ran terrible campaigns—perhaps they need to reevaluate their position on Trump. Mathematically, Kasich has been dead meat for weeks. If he had any dignity, he would quit, but he will not. Instead, he wants to try any manipulate the process to gain the nomination, despite the fact that he has been soundly repudiated by the people.

My candidate, Cruz, is on life-support and will be eliminated mathematically next Tuesday. I hope he is gracious and gets out of the race. There are a lot of conservatives who do not like Trump, but I can't believe any of them would prefer Hillary Clinton—who Trump has accurately deemed "Crooked Hillary."

Now, it's time to come together and heal the hurt feelings so many have. We must do this. It's our responsibility. After all, America is worth it. Our choice is either Trump or Crooked Hillary. I know which one will be best for America, don't you?

4/20

Bernie Needs to Stay in the Race
RCP: Clinton – 48.8 Trump – 39.5

COMMON SENSE: My advice to Bernie Sanders is the exact opposite of what I have suggested for Cruz and Kasich. Regardless of how substantial the lead Hillary has developed, Bernie should continue. The reason is an independent variable that the Republicans don't have—an FBI investigation.

Despite the fix probably being set by Obama and Loretta Lynch to keep Hillary from being indicted, it will be difficult to keep one hundred FBI agents silent about Crooked Hillary's crimes. When it comes out, and it will, Bernie needs to be there to pick up the pieces. So, keep running, Bernie. You may end up being the nominee, after all.

4/20

Trump Will Win on 1st Ballot

RCP: Clinton – 48.8 Trump – 39.5

COMMON SENSE: Because of what happened in New York, I believe Trump will win the nomination on the 1st ballot. My candidate, Cruz, couldn't even compete. So, all of this talk about what will happen on subsequent ballots is just a waste of time. Uncommitted delegates will be under enormous pressure to support Trump.

Although I did not see it coming, Trump is clearly the people's choice, and I plan to support him and not be an obstructionist. I suggest you do the same thing, even if you don't want to admit doing so publicly.

The media has done an excellent job of telling us Hillary will destroy Trump in the general election, but I don't believe this for one minute. There is tremendous enthusiasm for Trump and none for Hillary. Besides, her ethical problems may yet doom her candidacy.

I would like for Trump to be kinder—except for calling Clinton "Crooked Hillary." I like that. I would also like to see him appoint Ted Cruz to the Supreme Court. If that happened, Trump would make a lot of us happy.

Here is what I suggest. Let your anger go, knowing that defeating Crooked Hillary is essential for preserving our heritage and making America great again.

4/22

We Must Work Hard to Defeat "Crooked Hillary"

RCP: Clinton – 49.5 Trump – 40.3

COMMON SENSE: At this time in 1980, I was finishing my course work for my Ph.D. in Political Science at Emory University. Ronald Reagan was close to becoming the Republican nominee. All of my professors at Emory were thrilled with this, because the polls showed that Jimmy Carter, Georgia's own, would destroy Reagan in the general election.

At the time, I believed my professors were right, but I didn't allow that to stop me. I loved my nation more—still do. Consequently, I decided to tell everybody I met, while selling fashion shoes part-time at I. Miller, about why Reagan would be a better President than Carter. My professors continued to mock the people's choice, and the Republican establishment lamented the insanity of its own supporters—just like now.

The rest is history, and it's about to repeat itself. Our choice will be Trump or Hillary—Crooked Hillary. So, stop your whining, negative defeatism and make a commitment to get to work. We need to save this great nation. It can be done, but it will take a monumental effort to do so.

5/1

Hillary's Email Scandal Is a Criminal Investigation

RCP: Clinton – 47.4 Trump – 40.1

COMMON SENSE: Hillary Clinton consistently refers to the probe into her email scandal as a "Security Review," but the FBI does not do security reviews. They do criminal investigations. For her to refer to this as a security review is nothing more than trying to deflect from reality for political purposes.

The FBI granted immunity from prosecution to Bryan Pagliano— the man who created her email server. To obtain immunity, Pagliano had to give up his 5th Amendment rights. What are those 5th Amendment rights? Among other things, it is the right to not self-incriminate himself. By accepting this immunity, Pagliano and his attorney have made a de facto admission that what he did was criminal. If it wasn't criminal, he wouldn't need immunity from prosecution, would he?

If what Pagliano did was criminal, which the DOJ and FBI verified by offering him immunity, then wouldn't the person authorizing what he did also be guilty of criminal behavior? Obviously, the answer is yes. Hillary is behind this entire operation, which is a criminal investigation and, most assuredly, not a security review.

That the media does not connect the dots, like I have just done, shows that they are either incompetent or part of a vast Leftwing Conspiracy. Hillary guarantees that she will not be indicted. How can she do that? What does she know that we do not? And what is the involvement of the Obama administration in this? Will the Rule of Law prevail, or has a fix already been put in place? Can the Attorney General, Loretta Lynch, be compromised? Can the FBI? When will the criminal investigation be complete? Will justice ever be served?

Right now, there are far more questions than answers, but the truth will come out—rest assured of that. I just hope it does before the election in November. If not, Crooked Hillary may be able to pardon herself.

Here Is My Advice for Trump
RCP: Clinton – 47.4 Trump – 30.1

COMMON SENSE: If I were advising Donald Trump, this is what I would tell him to do. After winning Indiana on Tuesday, which is going to happen, I would thank Ted Cruz for running a spirited campaign. Then, I would never mention him again. I wouldn't even acknowledge Kasich.

I would shift all of my attention to Hillary, asking when the FBI's criminal investigation about her server and foundation would be made public. Put the pressure on them to be forthcoming. Make them be defensive. Doing this would generate a lot of coverage, and there is no downside to it.

Within a week or two, I would select Marco Rubio to be my running mate. This would assuage the miffed feelings of many conservatives and establishment Republicans too. After picking him, I would turn him loose in California, where his Spanish heritage is a real plus.

Once Trump gets to 1,237 delegates, which he will, I would allow Kasich to open up the Convention, since it's in Cleveland. By doing all of these things, he can start the healing process, while simultaneously putting Crooked Hillary on the defensive.

Trump Will Win in November: Here's Why

RCP: Clinton – 47.3 Trump – 40.8

COMMON SENSE: Trump will win in November. He will be our next President and Commander-in-Chief. Count on it. Despite what all of the talking heads tell you to the contrary, they are wrong. I am right about this; trust me.

Here's the reason why: Trump has the best political instincts I have ever seen—better than Reagan's, Bill Clinton's, or Barack Obama's. Because I did not take Trump seriously at first, I didn't see this, but it has become the most obvious characteristic of his campaign, once I started paying closer attention.

Hillary can't think on her feet, Trump can. Hillary can't pivot without massive scripting; Trump does this fluidly. Hillary, like her policies and thinking, is old and unsuccessful. Trump's ideas and style are new, innovative, and solidly anti-establishment.

Here are some of the things I think Trump should do in to enhance his position:

1. He should continue to stress how unfair the Democrats are being to Sanders by denying him equal distribution to their super-delegates, calling the system crooked and rigged. By doing this, it will continue to erode Hillary's position with Millennials. By the time Hillary gets the nomination, which is inevitable, there will be a gaping hole in the coalition that elected Obama twice.

2. Pick Rubio to be his V.P. Because Marco is liked and respected by both conservatives and RINOs, he can be indispensable in healing wounds with those who need to be in the Trump coalition. Once selected, send Marco to the Capitol to meet with Republican leaders. Then, turn him loose to get the Latino vote in Florida, California, New Mexico, New York, and New Jersey—all states that will be in play.

3. Start naming people who will be considered for a Trump cabinet position, using the example of Christie as Attorney General, Carson as Surgeon General, etc. By beginning to surround himself with respected and talented people, using the Reagan model of being Chairman of the Board, tepid and tenuous supporters will become enthusiastic.

4. Drop several names as possible Supreme Court nominees, including Ted Cruz. Because Cruz's supporters are all committed

Constitutionalists, they will see the value of a Cruz appointment, and the #NeverTrump movement will melt like ice cream in July.

5/5

Bush's Nixing Trump Is an Affront to American Voters

RCP: Clinton – 47.3 Trump – 40.8

COMMON SENSE: President Bush (43), for 7.5 years you have not spoken up about how Barack Obama has been systematically trying to destroy the United States of America. Now, after remaining silent for so long, you choose to be vocal—not about Obama's disastrous policies or Hillary's corruption—but about Donald Trump and your inability to support his nomination for President.

Maybe you were wise to not criticize Obama. If that's true, then you would have been equally wise to continue remaining silent. You haven't snubbed Trump as much as you have snubbed those who voted for you twice but are fed up with electing Campaign Conservatives—those who do not keep their promises to the American people once they have been elected.

Respectfully, Sir, I am very disappointed with you. Because of his age, I give your dad a pass.

5/7

Obama's Scolding of Trump Is Laughable

RCP: Clinton – 47.3 Trump – 40.8

COMMON SENSE: President Obama, our consummate dilettante, is now lecturing Donald Trump about how serious the office of the Presidency is. Talk about the pot calling the kettle black!

If you'll remember, Obama is the Commander-in-Chief who has skipped more than half of his daily National Security Briefings, each and every year he has been in office, while the threat of ISIS has continued to grow. Obama is so serious about his job that he was on the golf course eight minutes after informing the American people about James Foley's beheading in 2014. How can the admonitions of a President like this be taken seriously?

Far worse, we still don't know what he was doing, when the Consulate in Benghazi was attacked, and we still don't have a satisfactory answer about why help was never sent to save our men. But we do know what he did the day after, don't we? He flew to Las Vegas to party with Beyonce. To Obama, that was more important than doing his job.

Obama's incompetence and lackadaisical ways are well documented. That the fawning press refuses to call him on it isn't surprising, but I'm calling him on it now. You have been a disgrace, Mr. President, and you need to keep your mouth shut.

5/8

Endorsements Don't Mean Much in 2016

RCP: Clinton – 47.3 Trump – 40.8

COMMON SENSE: Frankly, I couldn't care less who endorses Donald Trump or not. Endorsements from the establishment are counterproductive anyway. This cycle, they will have virtually no impact.

I am interested in who endorses Hillary Clinton though. There are the men and women who may be complicit in her corruption, when she was allegedly was influence peddling, while being Secretary of State. I'll be even more interested in who President Obama pardons his last week in office. I'm interested in both of these lists. I'll bet Obama's list of those being pardoned is the largest in American history.

5/8

The Bush Family Should Be Ashamed of Themselves

RCP: Clinton – 49.0 Trump – 39.2

COMMON SENSE: So far, the posts I put up about Bush 41 and

43 refusing to supporting Donald Trump have been reposted on Facebook 1,555 times, and it has more than 1,700 likes.

On my blog, We Believe America, 2,200 people from all over the world have read what I wrote in the last two day, including people from these nations: Ecuador, Canada, Switzerland, Japan, UK, Mexico, Australia, Germany, Philippines, Malaysia, Bahrain, Puerto Rico, South Africa, Italy, Singapore, France, Ireland, and Israel.

I am just one guy, but we are making a difference—a big difference, worldwide. Politicians and media analysts cannot understand this movement, nor do they have a clue about how powerful it is. But they will. It's inevitable. We are taking our nation back from the politicians, and they can't stop us.

We Are Taking Our Nation Back from Politicians

RCP: Clinton – 47.3 Trump – 49.8

COMMON SENSE: In the Presidential Election, many news items are unimportant, but not all of them. Some things are very important—a few are critical. Take what Secretary of State John Kerry said to the graduating students at Northeastern University, for example. He told them that one day they would be living in a "world without borders," implying that this would be a good thing.

This is what the Progressives want—a world without borders. Having no borders means the United States would have to embrace whoever comes, regardless of who they are. In their desire to create a Utopian dream world, Progressives like Kerry, Obama, and Hillary Clinton abhor American nationalism, mocking those who desire strong borders.

To them, their worldview is sophisticated. Our belief system, by way of contrast, is outdated and doomed to fail. In the Progressive mindset, our military might be necessary, but honoring American soldiers or taking care of them is unimportant. Without borders, you would still need some policemen but not the Army or the Navy.

Because Donald Trump wants to "Make America Great Again," which is the exact opposite of what Obama, Kerry, and Hillary want, they loathe him. He espouses the exact opposite of what they desire for our future.

When you think of it like this, it's easy to see why they hate Trump so much, and will do anything to discredit him. As you can see, this is a critical issue—not a trivial one. If you believe in secure borders and want America to come first, choose Trump. If you want a world without borders, Hillary is your candidate. It's as simple as that.

3/21

More Welfare to Illegal Aliens than American Families

RCP: Clinton – 47.3 Trump – 40.8

COMMON SENSE: Illegal immigrant households receive an average of $5,692 in federal welfare benefits every year. This is far more than the average American family receiving assistance. On average, they receive $4,431, according to a new report on the cost of immigration released today by the Center for Immigration Studies.

Here is my question: Why are we paying anything for the upkeep of illegals? Why are they our responsibility?

5/10

If Quinnipiac Poll Is Right, Trump Will Beat Hillary

RCP: Clinton – 47.3 Trump – 40.9

COMMON SENSE: A new Quinnipiac Poll shows Trump winning Ohio and just 1 percent behind Hillary Clinton in two other battleground states—Pennsylvania and Florida. In 2012, Obama beat Romney in the Electoral College by a decisive margin, 332 to 206.

In 2016, if these three states that voted for Obama are flipped, the total would be—Trump 273, Clinton 265.

Since it takes 270 Electoral votes to win the White House, if every other state remains the same and these three key states are flipped, which is going to happen, Trump will be the next President of the United States.

As President, he will choose the judges for the Supreme Court and not Hillary Clinton. He will also be responsible for our economy and for ferreting out political corruption, including Hillary Clinton's.

5/12

Hillary Will Never be Indicted
RCP: Clinton – 47.2 Trump – 40.8

COMMON SENSE: When you are a Progressive, immutable truth does not exist; everything is relative. So, to Hillary Clinton, truth becomes what furthers her goals—nothing more, nothing less. With this as her standard, a criminal investigation into her illegal email server becomes a "security inquiry," making it no big deal.

It's no big deal because this is how she defines it, but it is a big deal to FBI Director, James Comey. He flat-out said the Bureau was doing an investigation, not a security inquiry. By the way, the FBI only does criminal investigations. They do not do security inquiries.

Hillary Clinton is in hot water up to her neck, but she probably will not be held accountable for her reckless disregard of the law concerning her email server, or for her corruption in influence peddling—nor granting favors while Secretary of State, in exchange for donations for her charitable foundation.

The reason she will not be held accountable is because power is more highly valued than truth for Progressives. If Hillary was a Conservative, where truth and probity are highly valued, her base would have already evaporated, and they would be calling for her indictment. But Hillary is not a Conservative; she's a Progressive. The rules for Progressives are different. Neither the Rule of Law nor the Constitution apply—only what works, meaning what gains and keeps them in power.

The bottom line is this: Hillary is guilty as sin, but the wages of sin is never death . . . not for a Progressive. She will never be held accountable for her criminal behavior—not by a Progressive administration. It's up to the people to see that justice is served. By voting against her, we can repudiate her, and this is exactly what we should do.

5/15

Romney's Attempted Coup Is Appalling

RCP: Clinton – 47.3 Trump – 41.6

COMMON SENSE: Four years ago, my first choice for President

was Newt Gingrich. He was clearly the most capable man, but Mitt spent a small fortune to destroy Newt in FL and take the nomination. In the general election, knowing how disastrous Obama had been, I supported Mitt, even though he was a very weak candidate.

Now, four years later, Mitt will not reciprocate and support the will of the Republican electorate. Although I voted for Cruz, I have no problem transferring my allegiance to Trump, knowing how disastrous Hillary would be as President. Why can't Romney do the same thing? Is his arrogance and self-importance so great that he cannot condescend to accept the will of the people? His behavior is appalling, as is Eric Ericsson's, and that little twerp from *The Weekly Standard*. I'm truly disappointed with them and will never support anything they ever do again.

Concervatives Should Embrace Trump
RCP: Clinton – 47.0 Trump – 41.8

COMMON SENSE: I voted for Cruz, but he lost. Eventually, he couldn't even compete. Now, I support Trump. In fact, I champion him. He may not be the Constitutionalist I desired, but he is a fearless advocate for the American people, and I'm tired of being led by a man who feels it is his duty to apologize for us.

I would rather have 75 percent of what I want than another four years of something I know I don't want. If Donald Trump secures our borders, rebuilds the military, and makes us energy independent, we will once again be a great nation, and he intends to do a lot more than that.

I exhort my fellow Conservatives to choose pragmatism over petulance and embrace the Trump candidacy. This patriot is offering a seat at the table of power, and we would be foolish to reject it in favor of some misguided sense of self-righteous purity. To choose the way of a fool, as Mitt Romney has done, will do nothing other than ensure Obama's legacy is preserved by the most corrupt woman in American history. Let's help make history rather than be a victim of it.

5/18

Trump Will Win in a Landslide
RCP: Clinton – 46.2 Trump – 42.3

COMMON SENSE: Donald Trump will win in November. In fact, I predict he will win in a landslide similar to Reagan's victory in 1980. Here's the reason why.

Hillary, the consummate political insider, is not only corrupt, but she also lacks personal appeal. There's nothing warm or inspiring about her, but here's the larger issue. The states she is winning—her "Firewall"—are all Red States. She stopped The Bern's momentum in the early primaries by winning South Carolina. Although this was heralded as a great victory for her, she has zero chance of winning South Carolina in the general election—just like she has zero chance of winning Alabama, Texas, Oklahoma,

Arkansas, Georgia, Tennessee, or any other solid red state.

The Bern is winning most of the Blue States. So, the places where she has to do well against Trump, Hillary isn't fairing well at all. The energy is all with Bernie—none of it is with her. With both Bernie and Trump articulating the same message—that the system is rigged to favor this unethical woman—those disaffected by this message will not embrace her. I doubt Hillary will be able to turn things around, even with a Sanders endorsement.

To young voters, Bernie's base, she is viewed as negatively as Trump supporters see her. Once the FBI's investigation is complete, which is imminent, and she is not indicted by Obama's DOJ, she will be universally castigated as Crooked Hillary—a name she richly deserves. Her credibility is shot. She might as well campaign by saying, "If you like your doctor, you can keep your doctor."

5/20

Releasing the 9/11 Report
Will Boost Trump

RCP: Clinton – 45.8 Trump – 42.7

COMMON SENSE: When the missing twenty-eight pages of the classified 9/11 Report are finally released, which shouldn't be long from now, both the Bush and Obama administrations are going to take a massive public relations hit. The American people are going to feel like they have been purposefully deceived for years by George W. and Barack, and they have. The outrage over this deception will be deafening.

Because she was Secretary of State during this time, Hillary's credibility and competence will be called into question once again—justifiably so. She had a role in this cover-up, and it's going to hurt her—but not as bad as Benghazi has. Trump, who is already up by 22 percent among men, will get another massive boost to his "outsider" candidacy. Because safety is a key issue, his negatives with women will diminish, as Americans of both genders come to realize that we need a massive purging of the status quo.

In words Trump might use, this is "going to be huge . . . Huuuge!"

5/24

Socialists and Progressives Will Never Defeat Trump

RCP: Clinton – 43.4 Trump – 43.2

COMMON SENSE: Socialists and Progressives—people like Obama, Kerry, and Hillary—have a fundamental flaw in their belief system. According to their way of thinking, which features a materialistic worldview rather than a theistic one, there is something missing in the lives of terrorists. Therefore, the way to end terrorism is to discover what the problem is, and find a way to provide a solution.

One non-theistic interpretation of the problem is this: Because of climate change, the Middle East is becoming uninhabitable. The terrorists are simply trying to fight their way out of the desert to find more suitable surroundings. So, the answer isn't to fight them; it's to find them a better place to live.

Leaders in our State Department, and many others in Europe, actually believe nonsense like this. It's what makes us as vulnerable as we are. Our greatest enemy isn't Jihadism; it's the flawed thinking of Progressives and Socialists.

At its core, Radical Islamic Terrorism is a theological problem. They want a worldwide Caliphate—one ushered in by the blood of Islamic martyrs. Until Sharia Law is universally accepted worldwide, they will not be satisfied. Because their traditional enemy, Israel, will never bow their knees and accept Allah as supreme, all Jews must die. The USA, the Great Satan, is next.

In 1492, when Columbus was discovering the New World, the Spanish monarchs, Ferdinand and Isabella, expelled all Muslims from Europe. Although history has not been kind to them for this, it's becoming increasingly clear why they did it, isn't it?

Twice before, the Islamic assault on the West has been stopped in its tracks, sending these barbarians back to where they belong. This feat was accomplished by those who understood that the problem was actually a war of belief systems—Islamism versus Judeo-Christianity. This hasn't changed. It's still the same fight, but the Progressives and Socialists don't have the capacity to understand it. Because they cannot conceptualize in terms like this, they are incapable of resolving the problem. With Progressives leading us, we will never be safe.

Muslim Jihadists understand brute force and nothing else. Playing nice, and trying to understand them, doesn't work. It never has, and it never will. It's also the reason why electing Progressives is self-defeating. If you want to be safe, you have to elect people who understand the problem, and Hillary certainly isn't one of them.

5/25

Closing GITMO Denies the Reality of Terrorist Threat

RCP: Clinton – 43.4 Trump – 43.2

COMMON SENSE: President Obama, fully intent on fulfilling his campaign promise to his Progressive base to shutdown GITMO, intends to release the mastermind behind the attack on the *USS Cole*. According to Obama and his Progressive cronies, GITMO's continuation gives ISIS a powerful recruitment tool, and we must not do that. At the same time, Obama and Hillary are pushing the Gay & Lesbian agenda full force, which obviously offends Muslims much more than anything else would.

Obama and Hillary want it both ways. They do not care about the 17 sailors killed that day or the 39 wounded—not like they care about pleasing the Leftists in Hollywood. After all, what difference, at this point, does it make?

5/26

Elizabeth Warren's Role Is to Show up Hillary

RCP: Clinton – 43.8 Trump – 42.8

COMMON SENSE: Has Elizabeth Warren really become a surrogate for Hillary Clinton? Or, is something else going on?

I suspect Warren has come out swinging against Donald Trump, hoping to scalp him, because the Democratic Establishment, beginning with its leader, is concerned that the legal issues facing Hillary Clinton may make her candidacy untenable. If I am correct, and I believe I am, this means Barack Obama is manipulating things from behind the curtain, fully intent on taking Crooked Hillary down.

Remember, the Inspector General's Report from the State Department came from the Obama administration—not a vast Right Wing Conspiracy. When you add the investigation of Governor Terry McAuliffe to the mix—a Clinton crony—a pattern is beginning to emerge. The FBI report about her email server will be next.

Pocahontas is not a friend of Hillary's, and the Obama's call the former Secretary of State, Hildabeast. I believe Obama secretly wants Hillary to go down, and he certainly has the power to make that happen. On the outside, Barack appears to be very supportive, but I do not believe he wants her to succeed him. At the same time, she has enough power to destroy Obama's legacy. So, he has to be very careful about how he undermines her, which explains the emergence of Pocahontas, who has certainly gone off the reservation.

If I am right, more bad news about Hillary will be forthcoming before the California primary. If it does, "The Bern" will win the state, and that will change everything about Hillary's viability. The Democrats cannot win the White House without California, and a Hillary loss will be depicted as putting the state in play for Trump. Her candidacy will collapse, including her Super Delegate support, but Bernie will not be the benefactor. Pocahontas, riding in on a pinto horse, will be tasked with doing that. A Native American will save the day for the Democrats, sparing the country from evil white men.

Stay tuned; the next few weeks should be a lot of fun.

5/29

Hillary Offers Bloated Bureaucracy– Trump Effective Business Principles

RCP: Clinton – 43.8 Trump – 42.8

COMMON SENSE: Hillary Clinton has 732 people on her campaign staff. Donald Trump has 70 to do the same thing. Hillary has more than ten times as many people employed than Trump, but his numbers are climbing, while hers are taking a nosedive.

The way the two are going about seeking the same office reveals the difference between how a career bureaucrat deals with a problem, as versus how a successful businessman does. Hillary has a huge, ineffective operation, while Trump has a lean, effective machine.

Since we are $20 trillion in debt, produced by spending good money wastefully, isn't it about time we began funding our limited resources more wisely? Our country is a mess, and the only way Hillary can solve a problem is to throw money at it—your money, by the way, not hers. We simply cannot afford another high-maintenance President. Any questions?

                      →

5/29

Hillary's Credibility & Trustworthiness Take a Big Hit

RCP: Clinton – 43.8 Trump – 42.8

COMMON SENSE: If you want to know what President Hillary Clinton would be like, just take a look at how she has handled this email server scandal. When caught, she lied.

Next, she had her server erased, saying there was nothing classified on it. When her deleted emails were retrieved, after an FBI investigation was launched, she lied; telling us it was nothing but a "Security Review." Again, this was a lie. It was a criminal investigation.

When the Inspector General asked for her cooperation with the State Department, she refused—so did her senior staff. Twenty-one out of twenty-six would not cooperate. Do you see a pattern here? Crooked Hillary has lied from day one and has continued to lie or deflect from her culpability throughout this entire episode.

Now that she has been caught red-handed, does she have any remorse? No! Is there any shame for her actions? No! Is there any repentance? No, instead, she has sent out her surrogates to "spin" her deception into something palatable—again deflecting from being transparent. Instead of being candid, she tells us her chicken you-know-what is really chicken salad.

America deserves better than this. Hillary Clinton is Evil, desperately wicked, shrill, and completely corrupt. If elected, we will have four more years of deceit coming from the White House.

6/2

Obama's Hidden Agenda for Hillary

RCP: Clinton – 43.8 Trump – 42.3

COMMON SENSE: After seven years of Barack Obama, I've learned one thing: Nothing is ever as it appears to be. A master of the slight-of-hand, Obama routinely deflects from his real agenda, as he blusters about things that are often unimportant, while accomplishing his nefarious goals in the dark, unimpeded.

Take his recent insertion into the 2016 Presidential Election for instance, where he has discarded tradition, by becoming active in his support for Hillary Clinton. On the surface, this appears to be one thing, but it may be quite the other.

Perhaps his support is feigned. He may know what the FBI's report on Crooked Hillary's racketeering reveals, and he is simply pretending to support her. This would provide political cover for him, as well as for his legacy. It would also allow him to feign surprise, when the DOJ chooses to bring the matter before a grand jury, ending the career of America's Medusa.

Or, Obama's support for Hillary may be a signal that the fix is in, and she can move forward, knowing that her corruption will never be prosecuted. With Obama, either scenario is possible. What is not possible, at least in my opinion, is that Obama will simply do the right thing and allow the chips fall where they may, as he took an oath to do, when he was inaugurated.

Hillary's Failed Foreign Policy
RCP: Clinton – 43.8 Trump – 42.3

COMMON SENSE: In Hillary Clinton's foreign policy speech, she said that Donald Trump's unpredictability makes him unfit to lead us in a crisis. On the other hand, we know exactly how Hillary reacts in a crisis, don't we? We don't have to guess.

In Benghazi, when the chips were down, Hillary didn't think about our ambassador or the others, did she? Instead of doing the right thing, which was to send help, she went into full cover-her-rear mode, joining our feckless President in concocting a lie about a You Tube video causing a spontaneous riot. Adding to their fabrication, Hillary's State Department bought TV ads in Pakistan—with your money—to try and spin their web of deception into the truth, but it hasn't worked.

Hillary is always self-serving. It's how she reacts in a crisis—no guesswork needed here. But that's not all. Because more than 600 requests for additional security coming from Ambassador Stevens were ignored by her State Department, we know she is either incapable of handling a big job or incompetent. By the way, where is the missing $6 billion from the State Department—lost under her watch? And how do you lose that much money?

What Hillary is good at is amassing a fortune by using her authority to sell favors to foreign governments. Her charitable foundation has close to $1.7 billion—much of the funds coming from foreign governments seeing favors—but she does use 6.4 percent of the funds to help others. The rest stays will Hillary, Bill, and Chelsea—bless their hearts.

When the full scope of what she has done to undermine this country becomes known, selling us out to the highest bidder, her place in history will be cemented. Her actions and egregious character flaws make her the one who is unfit to have the nuclear codes—not Donald Trump. Hillary, America's Medusa, personifies the worst character qualities of anybody who has ever run for the highest office in the land.

6/4

It's Time to Make a Stand for Righteousness

RCP: Clinton – 43.8 Trump – 42.4

COMMON SENSE: In American history, nearly every generation has faced a significant challenge—a moment in time, when good men and women have been asked to make a stand. This is our moment. For such a time as this, God has prepared many of us. It's now up to us to answer the call.

The future of our great nation is at stake. Depending on what we do or do not do, our destiny will unfold. I know what I am going to do.

I am fully aware that my choice for President is deeply flawed, but his goals are righteous; and he is willing to accept godly counsel. That's enough for me. Rather than curse the darkness like others, I intend to shine a light, knowing that the alternative is a devious woman who has a reprobate mind. Corrupt to the bone, under her leadership, the America we know and love will cease to exist.

The forces of darkness threaten to extinguish our light, but we do not need to allow this to happen. I know the Source of my strength, and I firmly believe that He is greater than anything that opposes us.

Now, the question is this: who will be strong and stand with me? Who will refuse to bow his or her knee to the god of this world?

Who is willing to pay the price to retake this great nation from the barbarians, the Progressives, and everyone else who is accursed?

6/7

Trump's Future Is in His Own Hands
RCP: Clinton – 44.0 Trump – 42.0

COMMON SENSE: Every Presidential campaign has gaffes and shaky moments. It's inevitable. The difference between successful candidates and unsuccessful ones is how they deal with these setbacks. In 2012, Governor Romney never recovered from his "47 percent" misstatement, as he fumbled away the election, never recovering. In 2008, however, Senator Obama was able to put the "God-Damn America" remarks of the Reverend Jeremiah Wright in the rearview mirror and get back on message, winning the election easily.

Now, in 2016, Trump's terrible blunder about the Mexican judge threatens to derail him, or he can learn from it and use its lesson to make him stronger, wiser, and more Presidential. Trump is best when he is larger than life—not when he succumbs to petty squabbling. If he can get back to who he is, painting a hopeful picture for the future, as many are encouraging him to do, he has the opportunity to do something truly great for America.

In his heart, I believe this is what he wants, but it is also very difficult for him to disengage from conflict, especially when he believes he has been treated unfairly.

Millions of us are rooting for him. He's all we have. He's our last, best hope to save us from being dominated by the depravity of Progressivism. If you haven't prayed for Donald Trump, it's time to get started.

6/8

Hillary, Bill, and Barack – the "Unholy Trinity of Depravity"

RCP: Clinton – 44.1 Trump – 41.0

COMMON SENSE: With only the FBI Primary to go, Hillary Clinton has won enough delegates to become the Democratic nominee for President. Because 75 percent of Democrats do not care if she is indicted or not, her email server issue—like so many other criminal activities—will be swept under the rug.

Now that she has the nomination, President Obama will endorse her. Breaking from tradition, his specialty, he intends to campaign for her vigorously—not because he likes her, but because he champions the darkness.

With her husband also campaigning, the three will become "The Unholy Trinity of Depravity," as they try gang up on Trump, trying to convince Americans that wrong is right.

If you are a political junkie, this is going to be fun. It's the fight of the millennium—The Corrupt Establishment vs. The Gunslinger. Despite it being three against one, if Trump can stay on message, he will be like "Blondie," taking out the villains in *The Good, the Bad, and the Ugly.*

Although Depraved, Hillary Could Win
RCP: Clinton – 44.1 Trump – 40.3

COMMON SENSE: Today, President Obama went to great lengths to endorse Hillary Clinton, going so far as to have a musical score backing up his scripted message. This means Donald Trump is not only facing Hillary, but he is also facing her husband and the sitting President. Essentially, Trump is running against "The Unholy Trinity of Depravity."

There is nothing these Evil people will not do to retain power—count on it. Based purely on her record, Hillary shouldn't have a chance, but she might win. It isn't just the Supreme Court that is at stake in this election; our entire way of life hangs in the balance. Because Hillary is corrupt, she will use every fraudulent trick in the book to ensure her victory. We must expect this and not be surprised when it happens. The voters must stop Hillary, who is a cancer on the soul of America.

Based on Obama's endorsement, I do not believe he will permit her to be indicted, as she should be. Instead, he will do everything in his power, which is substantial, to protect her from being held accountable for her criminal actions. This means it is up to us, the American people, to repudiate her and her deceitful ways. We have the power to do it, but we must not lose our resolve. If we do, the nation we will leave to our heirs will not be the great one our forefathers bequeathed to us.

Hillary Failed at the State Department
RCP: Clinton – 43.7 Trump – 39.2

COMMON SENSE: I find it interesting that Hillary Clinton is saying that her experience makes her more fit to be Commander-in-Chief, while simultaneously doing everything she can do to hide and mislead voters about her tenure at the State Department. Everything she put her hand to, while being our Secretary of State, failed. Nevertheless, because she held the job for four years, she must be a better choice for President than Donald Trump, right?

This convoluted logic just doesn't make sense. It's like asking Elizabeth Taylor to give marital advice. Having been married nine times, she must be an expert. Touting Hillary's experience uses the same logic, but it is flawed. Hillary failed at being Secretary of State, but she was successful at using her position of authority to make a fortune.

That it was accomplished at the expense of you, and every other American, is not her problem. Now, she is asking you to buy her deception and make her dream of becoming President a reality.

We should help her out, right? After all, it is a woman's turn to be President, isn't it?

6/12

ORLANDO: Gay Nightclub Attack
RCP: Clinton – 43.7 Trump – 39.2

COMMON SENSE: In Orlando, the attack killing 50 and wounding 40 was at Pulse—a gay nightclub. Yet, it wasn't until Peter Doocy of Fox News asked the question about Islamic Terrorism that the issue was addressed.

This underscores a fundamental problem in our politically correct society. Americans are so wed to Progressive thinking that they refuse to look at the obvious, for fear of being called Islamophobic.

This is a serious problem. I do not believe that Barack Obama, Hillary Clinton, or John Kerry want these kinds of attacks to occur, but the way they view the world simply does not allow them to deal with reality effectively. Because instances like these do not fit their political narrative, they spend more time reinterpreting what happens than addressing the problem.

Their politically correct worldview, which maintains Islam is a religion of peace and defies reality, makes us more ore vulnerable than we need to be, and it's why we desperately need a change in leadership. Hillary, who has a record of appeasing terrorism, simply cannot get the job done.

6/12

Neither Obama nor Hillary Can Deal with Terrorism

RCP: Clinton – 43.7 Trump – 39.2

COMMON SENSE: Beginning with the Fort Hood massacre by Major Nidal Hasan, one year into Obama's Presidency, the problem with Progressive thinking has been evident. Refusing to call his attack what it was, referring to it as "workplace violence" instead, because it fit Barack and Hillary's narrative, we have been made more vulnerable by our leadership than necessary.

Like a doctor who refuses to admit a patient has cancer, despite everything pointing to the contrary, the Obama/Hillary narrative has maintained the illusion that Islam is a religion of peace, when it is obvious there is a fundamental flaw with the Islamic Worldview.

To survive, we must stop the madness of believing the flawed tenets of political correctness. We must call a spade a spade and acknowledge that Radical Islamic Terrorism is real. San Bernardino and Orlando happened, but neither Obama nor Hillary is capable of dealing with it effectively. It's obvious.

In your heart, you know I'm right.

Obama Still Can't Call It Islamic Terrorism

RCP: Clinton – 43.7 Trump – 39.2

COMMON SENSE: While murdering 50 in Orlando, Omar Mateen yelled, "Allahu Akbar"—just like all other Muslim Jihadists do, when they are killing innocent people. Yet, President Obama used his news conference as an opportunity to push his gun control agenda, rather than address the real problem, which is Muslim terrorism. Obama didn't say one word about Muslim terror, despite this being the worst mass murder in American history. It's obvious Obama is incapable of acknowledging reality or dealing with it.

Neither is Obama 3.0—Hillary Clinton. How many more mass murders do we have to endure before we are willing to admit the problem is Radical Muslim Jihadism? Our President is supposed to keep us safe. It's his #1 job, but Obama is far more concerned with furthering his Progressive agenda on gun control than abiding by the oath he took to protect us.

6/13

Islamic Moderates Turn on the Radicals

RCP: Clinton – 43.3 Trump – 48.8

COMMON SENSE: Concerning the Orlando shooting, CAIR—the Congress on American-Islamic Relations—came out strongly against the radicals. So have many other Imams.

This is important, because we will never win the War on Islamic Terror without the support of moderate Muslims. They are the ones who need to be vigilant about radicalization. Non-Muslims can't do this nearly as effectively.

For the first time, moderates have ceased to be passive. If they continue to do this, it will make the FBI's task of ferreting out this Evil much easier. When the Jihadists turn on the moderates, which is inevitable, you will know we have turned the corner in this fight.

6/15

Yes, Naming "Radical Islamic Terrorism" Is Important

RCP: Clinton – 44.0 Trump – 38.4

COMMON SENSE: President Obama, who is a master at deflecting, tried to strike back at those who criticize him for not calling Radical Islamic Terrorism what it is. I'm sure multiplied millions will join him in mocking Donald Trump and people like me for making an issue about something Obama considers unimportant, but it is important.

First, it isn't just the term that is at issue. Through the Department of Justice's Civil Rights Division, Obama has a small army of doctrinaire Progressive lawyers who relentlessly impose Obama's worldview on America. Since Obama venerates Islam, nothing truthful that criticizes the "Religion of Peace" is allowed. Because this hampers our risk assessment of impending danger, Obama's delusional thinking about Islam's peacefulness makes us unsafe. Innocent people are dying because of this, and many more will follow.

Second, through the Department of Homeland Security, Obama and his sycophantic Progressive toady's have opened our boarders to allow undocumented militant Muslims into our nation by the thousands. This is a true Trojan Horse that will cause many needless deaths in the future. It's inevitable.

Third, Obama's justification for not calling Jihadism what it is, is that it would be a great recruitment tool for ISIS. Supposedly, it would give young Muslims a reason to hate us, which doesn't make a bit of sense. They already hate us. Instead of capitulating to them, which Muslims consider to be a sign of weakness—because it is—we need to be in their face constantly. That will work. Appeasement will not.

One more thing: Hillary, who has helped Obama get us into this mess, is now willing to call radicals what they are. This isn't surprising though. She will say anything or do anything to get elected—sleaze that she is.

6/18

Hillary's Story Defies Reality

RCP: Clinton – 44.9 Trump – 39.1

COMMON SENSE: If I had written a novel ten years ago about a corrupt woman, who gains the nomination of her party, while being investigated by the FBI for criminal misconduct, nobody would have believed the story line was plausible. If I added that the sitting President endorsed her candidacy, despite being fully aware that she made a fortune by leveraging her position as Secretary of State in a pay-to-play scheme that threatened national security, it would be a plot too far fetched to publish.

But, what if I added that this corrupt candidate also took the moral high ground over her opponent, deceiving millions with her duplicity? If I had written such a book, not even one publisher would have touched such an implausible story.

Yet, it is true, suggesting that truth is indeed stranger than fiction. God help us my friends, because it is quite clear we lack the wisdom and discernment to help ourselves.

6/19

Hillary and Obama Champion Depravity

RCP: Clinton – 44.9 Trump – 39.1

COMMON SENSE: The reemerging obsession with the O.J. Simpson case is very interesting. Like so many others, I can remember where I was, when the slow-speed chase happened and when the verdict was announced.

In many ways, that case reminds me of what is happening in our country today. When O.J. was acquitted, I was at the Varsity in Atlanta. All of the white people were stunned—shocked by such a miscarriage of justice—while the African-Americans cheered that he got off. Despite all the evidence to the contrary, they just wanted him to be acquitted.

It's the same thing in 2016. Our societal morality has declined so far that multiplied millions willingly support Hillary Clinton—the most corrupt politician in American history. Like O. J., they just don't care what she has done or how badly she has violated her oath of office. They just want to see a woman win.

It's the same with Obama. Fools by the millions excuse his deceit, his incompetence, and his loathing for the people he has sworn an oath to protect and defend. Progressives, blacks, gays, spineless Republicans, and those on the dole simply do not care that he has done everything in his considerable power to take the United States "down a notch or two." Calling right wrong, while they champion the wisdom of foolishness, with smug, self-righteous grins on their faces, like lemming racing to their inevitable demise, they are systematically destroying the foundations of our nation, which required centuries to build.

Equally at fault are many deluded Christians and Jews—those who should be able to discern this Evil, but are too compromised to do so. It's exactly like the Simpson trial. Just as I could not believe the verdict reached by O. J.'s jury, I cannot believe what I am seeing in America today. It's heartbreaking. I grieve for the future of our beloved nation.

6/21

Gay People Should Not Support Hillary
RCP: Clinton – 45.0 Trump – 39.2

COMMON SENSE: In the 1930s, anti-Semitism was very strong in Germany, but nobody was executed because of it. It wasn't until the Nazi's made it policy, using the force of the state, to kill Jews and homosexuals that the Holocaust began.

It's the same thing now. There is still anti-Semitism and anti-gay sentiment in the Western Democracies, but there are no executions because of it—no pogroms. In Muslim countries, however, where they practice Sharia Law, it's different. In Iran, for example, there are 75 million people but no gays—none. How could that be, you might ask? It's simple. Using the force of the state, where execution is legitimized, they execute gays—all of them—or at least as many as they can find. It's the same with ISIS.

Despite this, the Obama administration has been very supportive of Iran—Hillary too. Valerie Jarrett, his chief advisor, is Iranian. At the same time, without question or discernment, gays support Obama, Hillary, and the Democrats, never connecting the dots that this is not in their best interest. Perhaps it's time gays rethink their strategy.

6/23

The Gun Control Issue Is Sleazy Democratic Cynicism

RCP: Clinton – 45.3 Trump – 39.4

COMMON SENSE: In 2009 and 2010, the Democrats controlled the White House and Congress—both the Senate and the House. They could have passed as much gun legislation as they pleased. Having the Presidency and the Congress, they were unstoppable.

Do you know how many gun bills they proposed during those two years? None, Nada, ZIP. Back then, Col. Nadal slaughtered thirteen at Fort Hood. Why didn't their "outrage over guns" stir Obama, Pelosi, and Reid to action back then instead of now?

I'll tell you why. It's because they saw a political advantage . . . nothing else.

6/24

Something Is Fishy about the Orlando Investigation

RCP: Clinton – 45.3 Trump – 39.4

COMMON SENSE: Something is terribly wrong about the entire investigation into Omar Mateen's shooting at Pulse in Orlando, killing 49 people. I have some questions:

1. Why was Mateen's wife, who was an accomplice, allowed to flee? It's inconceivable that she wouldn't be under constant surveillance.

2. Why was every reference to Islam scrubbed from the original record?

3. From the retrieved record of the hostage's phones, Mateen was talking to a collaborator other than his wife. Who is it, and why have we not heard more about this?

Honestly, this is beginning to smell. Something is going on, and we don't have a clue what it is.

6/26

Hillary, Obama, and Kerry Emnable Terrorism

RCP: Clinton – 46.1 Trump – 39.4

COMMON SENSE: In recovery, an enabler is someone who misguidedly abets an addict, refusing to allow that person to face the consequences of his or her actions—like Hillary defending her sexual predator husband, Bill.

Likewise, every time Obama, Hillary, or Kerry refuse to call Radical Islamic Terrorism what it is, they become enablers for terrorists. They are providing these monsters cover, regardless of what their motivation might be. If every person in America understood this, nobody would vote for Hillary, Obama's approval rating would tank, and people would see Kerry for the fool that he is.

6/26

Where Is Omar Mateen's Wife?

RCP: Clinton – 46.1 Trump – 39.4

COMMON SENSE: Our leaders continue to promote the false narrative that they are in control and terrorism, particularly ISIS, is on the run. Yet, the Department of Homeland Security, the FBI, and the Orlando Police Department have lost track of Omar Mateen's wife, his accomplice in murdering 49 people at Pulse—the gay nightclub.

Where is she? What is being done to find her? And why isn't this a major news story? Is something fishy going on here? None of this makes sense to me. How about you?

6/27

Hillary's Strategy Versus Trump's
RCP: Clinton – 46.1 Trump – 39.4

COMMON SENSE: Here is my advice: Stick to your values and your determination to retake our nation from Progressives like Obama and Hillary. They will do everything they can to thwart our efforts, especially with the support of the sycophantic liberal media. For example, the ABC—Washington Post Poll that has Hillary ahead by 12 points is weighed heavily toward Democrats 2.5-to-1; but you never heard that, did you? The poll was purposefully skewed to shape public opinion, rather than reflect it, showing how dishonorable the media can be.

In the campaign, Hillary will spend $2 billion to paint Trump as unfit and dangerous, which he is not. She has to do this. It's her only card. She can't run on her record, since she has failed at everything she has ever done. Obviously, she can't run on her character, so all she can do is attack Trump mercilessly.

To win, Trump needs to stay on message, and it should be this: If you want four more years of global retreat, Hillary is your candidate. If you want to make America great again, vote for me.

If you want to see your wages lose buying power, while increasing our national debt to fund illegals, vote for Hillary. If you want "huge" growth, vote for me.

If you are content to be lied to, and are fine with denying the global threat of Radical Islamic Terrorism, choose Hillary. If you want the military restored and ISIS destroyed, vote for me.

If you don't mind working hard to barely make it, while the establishment elites become fabulously wealthy at your expense, vote for the most corrupt politician in American history, Hillary Rodham Clinton. If you want somebody who will work for free—just to make you better off—vote for me, Donald J. Trump.

6/28

Hillary's Strategy Against Trump Just Collapsed

RCP: Clinton – 45,8 Trump – 39.0

COMMON SENSE: Using carefully crafted phrases, each tested by focus groups, Hillary's campaign injects just enough truth, mixed with deceit and innuendo, to garner support from the naive, the ignorant, and the depraved—all to attack the character and qualifications of Donald J. Trump.

She intends to spend more than $1 billion, painting a word picture of Trump as being dangerous, reckless, and unfit to be Commander-in-Chief. By contrast, she purports herself to have the wisdom, experience, and steady hand to lead us in time of crisis.

Her strategy is impressive, except for one thing. It just fell apart at the press conference held by the Benghazi Select Committee, and the big winner is Trump. Without having to spend a dime in refutation of Hilary's massive campaign, the committee's report has done the work for him.

In a word picture, Hillary surmises what Trump might do in a crisis, and it isn't good. But what we now have are facts, showing that when a real crisis occurred under her watch, she didn't lift a finger to save American lives. Instead, while those brave men fought for their lives, Hillary's focus was on saving her political career, ensuring Barack Obama's reelection, and deceiving the American people about what really happened.

We know what kind of Commander-in-Chief she would make, don't we? She doesn't have the character qualities we need in a leader. Hillary is unfit to be President of the United States.

6/28

Hillary's Moral Depravity Is Unrivaled

RCP: Clinton – 45.8 Trump – 39.0

COMMON SENSE: During the Benghazi attack, the two unarmed drones flying overhead provided real-time intelligence to the White House, State Department, and Pentagon. This means that while Hillary was having meetings, planning on how to use the You Tube video to cover her rear, she had access to video that showed the fight was still going on—just like when she watched the attack on Osama bin Laden. Yet, when it came to our brave warriors in Benghazi, she did nothing to try and save them—nothing.

She let them die, never lifting a finger to help. She just didn't care. Hillary is cold. I've always known that, but what she did—or didn't do—shows a level of moral depravity that few can rival. She must never be our President.

6/29

Hillary Is Unfit to Be Commandar-in-Chief

RCP: Clinton – 45.1 Trump – 39.0

COMMON SENSE: Everybody knows that past performance is the best indicator for future behavior. That being said, while

Tyrone Woods and Glen Doherty were fighting for their lives, trying to hold on until help came, Secretary of State Hillary Clinton was huddled in the White House planning how to spin their deaths. Help never came of course, but Hillary did make up a good story. Her goal wasn't to save them but to deflect from her malfeasance and to ensure Barack Obama's reelection.

Now, four years later, despite all of her efforts to stonewall the investigation, we know exactly what happened. If she is elected President, she will throw our military under the bus to save her rear—just like she did at Benghazi. She is untrustworthy, consistently deceitful, and unfit to be Commander-in-Chief. That the Democrats would nominate her is shameful, but that they don't care what she did is even worse.

6/29

Something Is Fishy about Orlando Massacre

RCP: Clinton – 45.1 Trump – 39.0

COMMON SENSE: Seddique Mateen, father of the Orlando killer, Omar Mateen, has been a guest at Obama's White House and Hillary Clinton's State Department. I wonder what they talked about?

The senior Mateen, a supporter of the Taliban, is standing behind the President's podium in the White House Briefing Room. Apparently, Mateen has been a frequent visitor to the nation's Capitol. He has held meetings at Hillary's State Department. Doesn't this seem odd to you?

Hillary Clinton killed a Department of Homeland Security investigation related to Omar Mateen's mosque, the Islamic Center of Ft. Pierce—stopped the investigation dead in its tracks. She also made certain that the records were destroyed so that the case couldn't be reopened.

Now, Omar Mateen's wife, his accomplice has gone missing. But none of this seems to be newsworthy to the mainstream media, does it? All the press is interested in is using the attack to try and take away the 2nd Amendment rights of Americans. Hillary and Obama are using the massacre at Pulse to pound legitimate gun owners.

Why isn't someone in authority taking a look at oddities like this? There is definitely something fishy here, isn't there? This may well be our domestic Benghazi.

6/29

Obama, Fire Loretta Lynch Now!
RCP: Clinton – 45.1 Trump – 39.0

COMMON SENSE: So, Attorney General Lynch had a secret meeting with Bill Clinton on a private jet yesterday in Phoenix. If someone hadn't tipped off the press, we would never have known about it, would we? When asked about the topic of discussion, Lynch started feeding us a conk-n-bull story, saying they talked about their grandchildren. I certainly don't believe that, do you?

With so much at stake with the FBI's criminal investigation of Hillary, for the Attorney General to speak to the former President, especially in such a clandestine manner, is totally inappropriate.

It isn't good enough for Lynch to recues herself. Obama needs to fire her, but he won't, will he? No, of course he won't.

Now we know for certain that the fix is in. Once again, where the Clinton's are concerned, the Rule of Law means nothing. Even worse, this corrupt, deceitful Jezebel is leading in the polls. If Crooked Hillary becomes President, Lord help us.

7/1

Clinton and Lynch Have Cut a Sleazy Deal

RCP: Clinton – 44.6 Trump – 39.8

COMMON SENSE: If the meeting between Bill Clinton and Attorney General Loretta Lynch wasn't inappropriate—like Lynch and the Democrats are maintaining—then they shouldn't have any trouble answering the following questions:

1. Why was it secret? Why did it take investigative reporting by

the local ABC affiliate to bring it to light? Why did Lynch have to be "outed" before she admitted the meeting took place?

2. Why did the FBI and Secret Service insist there be no cell phones, recording devices, or cameras allowed in the vicinity? Who directed the FBI and Secret Service to make such an unusual demand, and why?

3. Why was the meeting held in an obscure location, if it was just social? Why was there such an air of secrecy about it?

4. If the "fix" for Hillary was not being set by Lynch, who was originally appointed to the federal bench by Bill Clinton, then why did the Department of Justice ask for a 27-month delay in producing the emails about the Clinton Foundation? Coming just two days after this clandestine meeting, this seems like quite a coincidence, don't you think?

5. Was this meeting completely accidental, or was it carefully planned? When did Lynch know that Clinton was going to meet with her? Is there any record of what was intended, or has this been scrubbed like everything else?

To take Bill Clinton at his word is something only a fool would do. Now that I've seen that Lynch fully intends to keep Americans in the dark, I will never trust her again. If anything, the pertinent emails about the Clinton Foundation should be produced immediately. The American people deserve to know what's in them before the November election. When you connect the dots, this whole thing stinks. Something is definitely wrong, and we need to find out what it is.

7/2

Slick Willie's Contribution to Trump's Campaign

RCP: Clinton – 44.8 Trump – 40.3

COMMON SENSE: I want to thank Bill Clinton for his contribution in kind to the Trump Campaign. At a time when Trump is behind in the polls and in fundraising, with many forecasting nothing but stormy weather ahead for the Trumpster, Bill's misstep, by compromising Hillary's email investigation, could not have come at a better time. At bare minimum, Slick Willie has done the following:

—Bill has added a new chapter to the lengthy book of Hillary's corrupt behavior and contempt for the Rule of Law.

—He has provided millions of dollars of free negative advertising directed toward Hillary's greatest weakness—her honesty and trustworthiness.

—He has also undermined the credibility of Obama's Department of Justice, marginalizing the Attorney General, Loretta Lynch, whose authority has just taken a massive hit.

—He has made it much more difficult for Hillary to attack Trump's character, knowing it will come right back in her face, as it should.

—He has single-handedly undermined all the efforts to coax Bernie's supporters into Hillary's camp, reinforcing their core belief that Hillary is Evil and corrupt to the bone.

For those of us who know exactly who Bill and Hillary Clinton are, from the bottom of our collective hearts, we thank you.

7/2

Hillary Testifies to the FBI, but Will Indictment Follow?

RCP: Clinton – 44.8 Trump – 40.3

COMMON SENSE: Thirty years ago, I was "interviewed" by the FBI. Although I was not the target of the investigation, let me assure you it caused the "Shrinkage Factor" with me—not swimming in cold water.

I promise you Hillary was squirming, and I wouldn't be surprised if she took the 5th. Remember, this is how they caught Slick Willie with his pants down about the Monica Lewinsky investigation. They knew things he didn't think they did, so they caught him in a lie. Hillary might have fallen into the same trap.

When Bill met with Loretta Lynch, he knew Hillary was going to be interviewed today. So did the Attorney General, but we did not. Bill and Hillary must have been terrified about this, which is understandable. It's what prompted Bill to "go off the reservation." Now, we know why he did, don't we? He needed to make sure the fix was still in for Crooked Hillary.

7/3

The Woman of Depravity Threatens Our Future

RCP: Clinton – 44.8 Trump – 40.3

COMMON SENSE: If you are a person of faith, character counts. It's why we hold our public figures to high standards, routinely rejecting them, when they reveal unacceptable flaws. We hold ourselves to lofty goals, and our leaders must also measure up to our expectations. We insist upon it.

People with a worldview not faith based have a different standard. Being materialists, they measure worth by what they have, or what they expect to obtain. To people like these, the ends justify the means. Having estimable character qualities isn't as highly valued as it is to people like us. They don't care. So, if a person can get away with something—regardless of how reprehensible it is—good for that person.

This is why there is no moral outrage over Hillary Clinton's conduct by her followers. They don't care that she is deceptive and corrupt. She can get them what they want, which is power, and that's all that matters to them.

In our history, this isn't the first time that the corrupt, the depraved and the reprobate have threatened to overwhelm our republic, but each time in the past, people of faith have rallied to steer the nation back to solid ground. Now, it is our turn. We have the opportunity to be strong and faithful. If we are, America will once again be a beacon of light for the entire world to emulate. If we falter and fail, our once great nation will sink into the abyss of mediocrity, depravity, and self-defeating behavior.

Which direction will we choose? What will the outcome be? Only God knows. The lines are drawn, and the sides are clear. Where do you stand?

7/3

Trump Has Many Positive Characteristics

RCP: Clinton – 44.8 Trump – 40.3

COMMON SENSE: I've been challenged to say something positive about Donald Trump, rather than just continue to point out how corrupt Hillary Clinton is. So, here goes:

1. Although Trump is not a traditional Christian, his love of country is very attractive. He genuinely wants to make America great again and has been willing to take millions of dollars worth of vicious ads aimed at him—both from the Right and the Left. He's doing this for us, and I admire him for it.

2. Compared to Barack Obama, Trump is a very strong man— one our allies will respect and our foes will fear. Unlike Obama, Trump will do what he says he will do, rather than behave like

Phineas T. Bluster.

3. Trump is committed to work for free. With Hillary selling favors to foreign nations—all to benefit her personal wealth—Trump will do the exact opposite. Running for President has cost him plenty. We can count on him to do the right thing for the right reason at the right time.

4. Trump will create real wealth for America and make our military stronger—both of which we desperately need after being raped by Team Obama.

7/4

Hillary's Nature Is to Be Untrustworthy

RCP: Clinton – 44.3 Trump – 39.2

COMMON SENSE: Hillary Clinton has announced she is going to address the issue of being untrustworthy. That's great news, but what does it mean? The easiest way to do this would be to come clean about all of her lies, beginning during the Watergate era, and apologize for being so deceptive, making a commitment to never lie again, regardless of the consequences.

But this isn't what she means by addressing her untrustworthiness, is it? Do you even believe she is capable of being honest? Is it in her nature to be straightforward, or is she so depraved that this isn't even possible? Perhaps our greatest problem is that so few even care that she has a reprobate mind to accompany her crooked behavior.

By addressing the "Trustworthy Issue," this is what she intends to do. She will assemble a focus group to determine what words make her appear to be honest and trustworthy, and which ones do not. Taking the group's advice, she will moderate her words—nothing else.

For better or worse, Hillary will never change. All she desires is the appearance of being trustworthy—not the actual character quality. Fraud, manipulation, deceit, and corruption are what she knows, and she will practice these damnable traits for the rest of her life. You can count on it.

7/5

Hillary Is Attempting to Bribe Loretta Lynch

RCP: Clinton – 44.9 Trump – 40.3

COMMON SENSE: According to a report from *The New York Times*, Hillary Clinton is considering retaining Loretta Lynch as Attorney General if she wins the presidency. Am I the only one who sees a problem with this?

To even suggest this is a blatant attempt to try and influence Loretta Lynch from indicting Hillary. How can it be seen any other way? There's nothing subtle about it either. It's a brazen—in our face— attempt to corrupt the Attorney General, by offering her a bribe.

Just as bad is the President campaigning for Hillary on the campaign trail. Normally, this would be fine, but not when the FBI is investigating her criminal behavior. Again, this is a brazen move, aimed at putting pressure on the FBI and the DOJ not to indict.

These actions aren't about politics. They are about right and wrong, following the law or skirting it, justice versus ratifying corruption. If you are not appalled by what is happening, you are not paying attention.

7/6

Hillary Is a Cancer on Our Soul
RCP: Clinton – 45.4 Trump – 40.6

COMMON SENSE: Hillary Clinton's egregious character qualities—deviousness, deceitfulness, incompetency, and corruption—make her unfit to be President. Anybody with a shred of decency and an intact moral compass knows this. There are enough good people to deny Hillary the Presidency.

Instead of being angry or discouraged that the Rule of Law does not apply to her, make a conscious determination to channel your energy to defeat her. We must do everything in our power, which is greater than you think, to make sure she does not win on November 8th.

There are still 125 days until the election. Make a commitment to contact 100 people in your sphere of influence, telling them we need to rid our nation of this metastasized cancer of corruption in our political soul, by choosing Trump over Clinton. If good people will do this, we can make sure Hillary is never President. Make the commitment to work for this today.

Together, we can make a difference. Our nation is worth saving. Join me, and let's turn things around.

7/7

Hillary Is Above the Law
RCP: Clinton – 45.6 Trump – 40.9

COMMON SENSE: Once again, the Clintons have beaten the system. When you were in school, do you remember how proud you were that nobody was above the law—not in America? Realizing this is no longer true is disheartening, isn't it?

Many feel like giving up, capitulating to corruption, believing that all is lost, but that isn't true—not unless we allow it to be true. Now is the time to step up—not retreat. Now is the time to make your voice be heard—not slink away in defeat. Now is the time to take our nation back from the corrupt politicians who have made a mockery of the Rule of Law.

It's our turn to stop being victims and take the fight to them. Be brave, regardless of what is required of you. America is worth it.

7/8

The Threat Is Terrorism
Not the 2nd Amendment

RCP: Clinton – 45.6 Trump – 40.9

COMMON SENSE: Another week, another attack, and another call by our tone-deaf, feckless President to disarm. Thanks to his misguided loyalty to everybody other than Americans, we are going to face repeated attacks for the foreseeable future. The enemy is among us, and only the most obdurate refuse to admit this obvious fact.

At a time when the need for personal safety has never been higher, Obama, Hillary, and the Progressives want to disarm us. We cannot allow this to happen. To survive, we must not permit them to eviscerate the 2nd Amendment. Now, more than ever, being American requires us to be strong.

7/10

Comey Has Comprimised the FBI

RCP: Clinton – 45.4 Trump – 40.9

COMMON SENSE: When FBI Director James Comey was asked if Hillary Clinton had lied during her interview, Comey said, "No." Technically, he answered truthfully but not honestly. Let me explain.

When Hillary, who was the target of a criminal investigation, was interviewed, she was not sworn in, like you and I would have been. Since she wasn't, nothing she said was technically a lie, meaning that perjury wasn't an issue. So Comey, who was sworn in, didn't lie to Congress, when he answered the question, but he wasn't transparent either.

Hillary's interview wasn't recorded. Nor were any notes taken, so we have no idea what happened; and we never will. This was by design. Comey, who testified about the FBI interview, wasn't even there.

Although Comey has called for "extraordinary transparency," he has been anything but forthright. I did not think the FBI could be compromised. Obviously, I was wrong, which is disheartening. What he has done has tarnished the FBI with corruption, making it no better than the IRS, DOJ, VA, and EPA.

The level of corruption that now exists in our country is beyond anything I have ever seen in my lifetime. The America I knew as a child no longer exists, but it doesn't need to remain this way. We can take our country back, and we must.

7/12

Lynch Stonewalled Congress – The Fix Is Set

RCP: Clinton – 45.4 Trump – 40.9

COMMON SENSE: If there was any doubt that a "Fix" has been set for Hillary, then Attorney General Loretta Lynch's testimony should confirm to you your worst suspicions. Lynch sat there, under oath, and stonewalled the committee, providing them with her carefully crafted response, and nothing more. She said the same thing so many times that it seemed like her mantra.

There was no explanation. There was no transparency. There was no remorse or anything aimed at being forthright. She is a lawyer, and she parsed her words carefully, refusing to be honest with the committee or the American people, which is her duty.

Right before our eyes, the Rule of Law has been mocked. With Bernie endorsing Hillary this morning, our nation is being hijacked, right out from under us. All that stands in the way for Evil to triumph is for the people to vote Crooked Hillary into office.

Will we? I don't know, but I do know this: Our nation is in peril.

7/14

Jeb Bush Is No Better Than Hillary
RCP: Clinton – 44.0 Trump – 40.9

COMMON SENSE: I believe Ted Cruz will endorse Donald Trump. He will do this because he said he would, and keeping his word is more important than anything to Senator Cruz. I do not expect Jeb Bush to keep his word. He has said that it would "violate his conscience" to vote for Trump, but what about us? He gave his word to us that he would support the nominee, didn't he? He even signed a pledge that he has no intention of honoring.

Bush's word doesn't mean a damn thing. It's not much better than Hillary's. It's also why he was a colossal failure in the primaries. His political career is over, as it should be. We do not need people like him—those who speak out of both sides of their mouth. I feel the same way about Senator Graham and Governor Kasich.

If Cruz fails to come through, even though I voted for him, I will be equally critical. Trump is our nominee, and I intend to support him vigorously. I suggest you do the same thing.

7/14

Comey and Lynch Threaten Investigation of FBI Agents

RCP: Clinton – 44.0 Trump – 40.9

COMMON SENSE: The FBI and Department of Justice are so worried that the truth will come out about their sleazy deal to protect Hillary that they have made the investigating agents sign a secret non-disclosure agreement about what really happened. Loretta Lynch and James Comey went to far as to say they would polygraph any agent even suspected of divulging the truth about what really happened.

In defiance of "Whistle Blower Protection Laws," Comey and Lynch have promised to destroy the careers of agents who just want to tell the truth. Obviously, the stakes in this game of deception are high, but the truth will eventually come out; it always does.

In the meantime, the perception of wrongdoing is relentlessly working against Crooked Hillary—a sobriquet she richly deserves. Her web of deception has become a tapestry, reminding us of who she is, who she has always been, and who she will forever be. She loves the darkness rather than the light, because her deeds are Evil.

7/14

Lynch & Comey – Criminal Conspiracy or Not?

RCP: Clinton – 44.0 Trump – 40.9

COMMON SENSE: Senator Grassley (R-IA) has a letter confirming that the FBI agents investigating Hillary's email scandal have been sworn to secrecy. When Comey said that this case demanded an "extraordinary amount of transparency," he was playing a shell game with the American people. He was not being straightforward.

I think Grassley should subpoena the investigating agents of the FBI directly, put them under oath, and ask them what happened. It's the only way to discover the truth. Their testimony before Congress supersedes the Non-Disclosure Agreement they signed.

Concurrently, Representative Chaffetz should do the same thing in the House of Representatives. Let Representative Trey Gowdy ask as many questions as he wants.

Attorney General Lynch and FBI Director Comey are involved in a vast Left-Wing conspiracy to undermine the Rule of Law and impact the 2016 Presidential Election. Their careers are over, and Hillary's scheme to thwart justice is coming apart at the seems.

7/15

Obama's and Hillary's Legacy Is Failure

RCP: Clinton – 43.1 Trump – 40.1

COMMON SENSE: Barack Obama began his Presidency by receiving the Nobel Peace Prize—not for what he had done but for what he was going to do. Teaming with Hillary Clinton as Secretary of State, this dynamic duo hit the "Reset Button," not only with Russia but also in the Middle East. Bolstered by their erudite Progressive worldview, the United States finally had the leadership we needed to right what was wrong and usher in a more equitable system—the New World Order.

Now, as Obama's second term is about to expire, instead of marveling at his accomplishments, we have to shake our collective heads at what a monumental failure he has been. The Middle East has destabilized dramatically, except for Iran, where they are busy producing nuclear weapons to destroy Israel and us—thanks to Barack Obama. Russian imperialism has ramped up considerably, and the European democracies are being destabilized by Radical Islam, which neither Obama or Hillary have the ability or moral courage to oppose adequately. All they can do is bluster, which they do routinely.

With Obama dancing the tango and Hillary selling favors to the highest bidder, our republic is being threatened by an Evil Wing of Islam that our leaders refuse to acknowledge even exists. Despite this, in his mind, Obama believes he has earned his Nobel Peace

Prize, and Hillary is making plans to extort one for herself.

We can stop this nonsense dead in its tracks, of course, but will we? Or, will we continue on the path of certain destruction by arguing about how many angels can dance on the head of a pin?

7/17

The Lawlessness We Are Experiencing Is Predictable

RCP: Clinton – 43.8 Trump – 40.9

COMMON SENSE: Behavior has consequences; so does a flawed belief system. After seven and one-half years of Obama's contempt for law, fostered by his Progressive beliefs that have undermined our republic, we are experiencing more lawlessness than we have in decades. Only a fool, or someone with a reprobate mind, would deny this obvious truth.

Equally destructive is how we champion leaders who mock the law, following those who think the law applies to the masses but not to them. Because Hillary scoffs at the Rule of Law, so do many others. Now, our chickens have come home to roost. We are experiencing the predictable penalty for being led by fools. As Americans, we are suffering the consequences of our corporate mistake. We were unwise to elect Obama twice; let us not replicate our error by electing Hillary.

7/20

The Battle for America's Soul Is on!
RCP: Clinton – 43.9 Trump – 40.1

COMMON SENSE: It's time to pivot our focus. Forget about trying to win over the #NeverTrump people. Some will eventually come around, but most will remain bitter. They prefer it that way.

It's time to conceptualize this campaign as a movement. It's an epic battle for the heart and soul of America, fought between the Children of the Light and the Children of Darkness. This doesn't mean that all of us are good and all of them are bad, but it does mean we have an entirely different way of looking at life.

We believe in American exceptionalism; they believe that the USA is responsible for most of the world's problems. We are strongly patriotic; they are ashamed of our nation. We believe in God; most of the Children of Darkness do not. We believe in personal responsibility, while they believe the ends justify the means. We want to make America great again, while they mock this idea. They are convinced America was never great in the first place.

The Children of Darkness support Hillary Clinton. Because their deeds are Evil, they have a vested interest in desiring the darkness her success will bring. Because their numbers are legion, it will require each of us to be strong. We must stand firm and never again be intimidated by their contemptuous mocking.

We will bend our knee to Almighty God but never to the will of the

Children of Darkness. For such a time as this, we have been pre-pared. Will we prevail, or will we be the generation that is respon-sible for the lights going out on the City on the Hill? The answer is in our hands.

7/21

Cruz's Bitterness Has Destroyed His Future

RCP: Clinton – 44.0 Trump – 41.3

COMMON SENSE: Bitterness is hardened anger. Nobody wants to be bitter, but it's inevitable, when you succumb to self-righ-teously embrace your wounds—when you justify them as being right—rather than turn them over to God. If you place them in God's hands, over time, you can become a forgiving person. If you can muster the courage to do this, you will become a per-son of value, a person who demonstrates the positive fruits of the Spirit of God.

Unfortunately, few choose to forgive. Because they do not own enough of their own souls, people like this chafe instead. They continue to justify their wounded-ness rather than abandon it. By embracing their acrimony, they think they are hurting the other person, but they are only hurting themselves. Unwittingly, they al-low emotional poison to become self-consuming, destroying their future.

Ted Cruz demonstrated this error for us last night. Does he have justification to be bitter? Of course, he does, but his actions only hurt him—not Donald Trump. I hate that this has happened, but it has. Like all of Life's lessons, I hope Cruz learns from it, but I doubt he will. Instead, like millions of others, he will choose to justify his actions, which are so unlike the Lord, Cruz talks about serving.

7/24

Trump Is Right – the System Has Been Rigged

RCP: Clinton – 44.7 Trump – 43.3

COMMON SENSE: Although I have consistently written about the political corruption in the Capitol, I'm even surprised by how deep it goes. Not only has Hillary skated on her email server scandal—thanks to the FBI and DOJ—but we now learn about how the DNC has rigged the system to ensure she received the nomination. Adding insult to injury, many of the GOP's most notable leaders actually favor Hillary over their own party's nominee.

Trump is right. The system is rigged. There is only one thing that stands in the way of Evil's complete triumph—you, the American voter. Will you sustain this massive assault against our core values, or will you rise up collectively, in righteous indignation, and say, "No!"

Will we coronate the Queen of Corruption, or will we put an end to her deceit and influence peddling? Will we sit by passively, as the values of our Founding Fathers are swept aside in favor of Progressive Socialism, or will we repudiate this Tsunami of Evil? Will we justify corruption, saying it's always present, or will we insist that the Rule of Law make everybody accountable, as our founders envisioned?

The answers are yet to be determined, but we will soon know—that is, if the voting machines have not already been rigged.

7/25

Dirty Debbie Is Out!
RCP: Clinton – 44.1 Trump – 44.3

COMMON SENSE: Dirty Debbie is out. She got fired for being unethical, which certainly shouldn't surprise anybody, especially Bernie's supporters. She even tried to use his Jewish heritage against him—a definite No-No for Democrats. But don't worry about Dirty Debbie. She has landed on her feet, thanks to the benevolence of Hillary Clinton.

Clinton says that Wasserman Schultz will serve as honorary chair of her campaign's 50-state program to help elect Democrats around the country. So, Dirty Debbie has a new job—actually a key appointment in the Clinton campaign.

But why would Hillary hire Dirty Debbie, especially now, when the full impact of her duplicity is yet to be unraveled? Doesn't that seem risky for Hillary?

Of course, it does, but Hillary probably had to do it. After all, the Queen of Corruption doesn't want Dirty Debbie to give a "Tell All" press conference, does she? Once again, someone is being thrown under the bus to protect Hillary. Unbelievable!

7/27

Trump Was Right About Russia Posting Hillary's Emails

RCP: Clinton – 44.6 Trump – 45.7

COMMON SENSE: If Donald trump suggested that Russia get involved in disclosing Hillary's 30,000 missing emails a month ago, even in jest, I might have been as enraged as the Left-Wing Media. But that was before I knew the FBI and Department of Justice could be compromised. That was before I knew the "Fix" was in for Hillary, and she would not be indicted, regardless of how egregious her behavior has been.

Until I witnessed Hillary walk, when she should have been indicted, I was still foolish enough to believe in the Rule of Law. I also believed nobody was above the law, but that's not true either.

I no longer believe either of these things because they are no longer true.

So, if Russia has the missing 30,000 emails, I hope they post them on WikiLeaks—I really do. I love our nation, but I am appalled by the depth of corruption in the Obama administration. I'm equally offended by Hillary, her foundation, and the establishment Republicans who willingly look the other way. I want them exposed—all of them, particularly the Queen of Corruption.

Hillary loves the darkness rather than the light because her deeds are Evil. If it takes Russia to expose her, then let it be. I want the truth—no matter what.

7/29

Hillary's Acceptance Speech Shows How Cunning She Is

RCP: Clinton – 44.3 Trump – 44.3

COMMON SENSE: Tonight, as the Democratic National Convention closes, you will be subjected to world-class sophistry. Hillary will present herself as a calm, safe, trustworthy, and honest Presidential candidate—a woman you should choose to be our leader. Each word she speaks will have been carefully tested for effectiveness. Each phrase she uses will has been scrutinized by focus groups to maximize their impact.

This is how Hillary plans to counter her high negative numbers on trust and honesty. She has chosen verbal seduction, rather than what is really needed, which is straightforwardness.

The worst part is there will be millions who embrace her falseness as truth and her cunning as caring.

Hillary Has Created an Illusion About Who She Is

RCP: Clinton – 43.7 Trump – 43.3

COMMON SENSE: Why would Hillary Clinton make the Democratic National Convention be about positioning her as the reincarnation of June Cleaver—Beaver's mom? Scripting everybody to fall into line with the theme that Hillary is a wonderful—albeit a misunderstood woman—speaker after speaker extolled her as a virtuous lady, someone who is warm, compassionate and giving. It was a great production. Unfortunately, it has nothing to do with reality.

The reason she chose this approach is because it's her default position on everything. When she is cornered, she lies. It's not just what she does; it's who she is. So, it's not surprising that she would use the DNC to create an illusion of who she thinks the American people want her to be. In fact, it's predictable. The last thing she wants is for you to know what she is really like.

Donald trump complains that she hasn't given a news conference in nearly nine months, but I think that, by not doing so, this is the most honest thing she has done. Since she will not give straightforward answers to direct questions—not without lying—why bother to go through the motions, knowing it would be a charade?

Because she will get much further by promoting the illusion of who she is, rather than letting us have a candid look at her, the Queen of Corruption will continue to extol her virtues—none of which square up with reality. It's her only option—her default position on everything. So, if you can stomach four more years of deceit, she's your gal.

7/31

Our Grass Roots Efforts Will Defeat Hillary

RCP: Clinton – 44.5 Trump – 43.4

COMMON SENSE: This campaign cycle, both parties had insurgency candidates—the Democrats an Independent and the Republicans a non-politician. The difference is the Republicans chose an outsider, while the Democrats doubled down on their establishment candidate. This means America has a real choice this year—not a slight nuance of difference, like most elections, but a real choice.

Because Hillary Clinton cannot run on her accomplishments, which are negligible, despite being a public figure since the Watergate hearings—where she was fired for being unethical—she has to paint Trump, the insurgency Republican, as temperamentally unfit to serve. Despite the fact that she has anger issues, Hillary will spend $2 billion in ads attacking Trump, while never pointing out what she has actually done, other than become filthy rich through corruption and influence peddling.

Aiding her efforts, the media will do everything it can to make Trump look like a fool. In Trump's favor is the social media—people like you and me. Because our goals are not self-serving, our influence is disproportionately greater than slick ads aimed at painting a deceptive picture.

If we stand strong and remain firm, we will restore our nation and end the corruption that threatens to destroy us. We are this strong; I promise we are. There are 99 days left before the election, use them wisely.

8/1

Khan Is Another Con Job by Hillary
RCP: Clinton – 45.9   Trump – 42.0

COMMON SENSE: Apparently, Khizr Muazzam Kahn, who was the most powerful voice at the Democratic National Convention, when he spoke about the death of his son in Iraq in 2004, is not who he says he is. Although he holds up a copy of the Constitution and tells us he supports it, he is actually a member of the Muslim

Brotherhood and wants to impose Sharia Law in America.

Aided by the fawning voice of the mainstream media, this is just another con by Hillary Clinton and her campaign, and millions of Americans have been fooled by it—just like always. The entire Convention, which tried to paint the Queen of Corruption as Mother Teresa, was deeply cynical, divisive, and deceitful. Although Khan's delivery was powerful and his loss was legitimate, his patriotism was a sham. Sharia Law is antithetical to the Constitution.

8/1

Three Things Trump Must Do to Win
RCP: Clinton – 45.9 Trump – 42.0

COMMON SENSE: If the upcoming election is a referendum on Hillary Clinton being deceitful, corrupt, and incompetent, she will lose. She knows this, so she is making the election a referendum on Donald Trump, spending up to $2 billion to make him appear unfit to be Commander-in-Chief.

To counter her cynical strategy effectively, Trump needs to do three things:

1. Stop falling into the traps set for him, which take him off message.

2. Develop a list of 10 things he will do within the first 100 days after being inaugurated, and hammer it home daily.

3. Announce the team he intends to have around him, and make it as strong as possible.

If Trump keeps on message, he can win. If he doesn't, we are in deep Bandini.

8/4

Putin Wants Hillary to Win, Not Trump

RCP: Clinton – 47.4 Trump – 40.6

COMMON SENSE: The narrative is being put forward by the media that Vladimir Putin wants Donald Trump to win the election, so the Russian dictator is doing whatever he can to manipulate the election toward this goal. But ask yourself this question: Why would Putin do this? What would he have to gain from it?

Trump is strong and unpredictable—not easily intimidated like Obama has been. Since Putin wants to reassemble the lost parts of the Soviet Union, would having a strong leader in the White House be to his advantage. Of course it wouldn't.

If Hillary is elected, would Putin be better off? Like Obama, she is weak and inept, but that is not what Putin likes the best about her. It's her corruption that he desires, knowing it will be easy to manipulate her. If the Kremlin has her emails, which we all know they do, he can blackmail her into doing whatever he wants. Because she has already been compromised, she will be putty in his hands, and the world will be destabilized further.

So, the narrative that Putin wants Trump to win is false. That our media cannot see through this speaks volumes about their ability to do their job. The message probably originated from the Clinton Campaign.

The world is much safer with a strong America, which Trump will produce—not Hillary Clinton.

8/6

Khan's Speech at the DNC Set a Trap for Trump

RCP: Clinton – 47.3 Trump – 40.4

COMMON SENSE: When Khizr Khan spoke at the Democratic National Convention, it was the most powerful moment of the evening, but it was an entirely manufactured event. The only real thing about it was the sacrifice of his brave son dying in Iraq in 2004.

The Clinton campaign set a trap for Donald Trump, and he walked right into it. The polls show that 79 percent of Americans disapprove of Trump's handling of Khan, but it was nothing more than a "Dirty Trick" by Clinton, which shouldn't surprise anybody. Here are some things about the incident that you probably do not know:

– Khan was paid $25,000 by the Clinton campaign to speak at the

DNC. Some say he was paid as much as $375,000.

– The speech was not written by Mr. Khan, but by two campaign staffers.

– The copy of the US Constitution that Mr. Khan held up was given to him two hours before his speech by a female staffer. It was a prop used by Khan and returned after speaking. The graphics are off center, and the word "Constitution" was not capitalized, showing that it wasn't a real copy of the Constitution.

– 5 Gold Star families turned down the opportunity to speak before Khan was contacted by the Clinton campaign.

– All five families were paid $5,000 and signed a non-disclosure agreement.

– Khan's immigration law firm is in debt $1.7 million and owes back taxes of upward to $850,000, plus penalties.

– CNN paid Khan over $100,000 to tell his "story," and he has repeated it in interviews worldwide.

– Khan was given a bonus of $175,000 by the DNC for his effort in the media.

– The IRS has since put Khan's tax file on "hold"—a reward for how well he did.

—Khan is taking his message worldwide, saying that Allah is destroying Trump's campaign.

That Trump stepped into this trap is regrettable. It has cost him dearly, but he was set up by the Clinton campaign. Unfortunately, the truth about this will only be known by a few, and we will be mocked for saying it.

Trump, It's Time to Get Strong
RCP: Clinton – 47.5 Trump – 40.5

COMMON SENSE: What amazes me it this: Hillary Clinton is a criminal. She should have been indicted for what she did and for her role in the pay-to-play scheme of the Clinton Foundation, but that hasn't happened. Yet, the entire Democratic machine is behind her. There isn't anybody saying they will not vote for her because she is a "flawed" candidate, which she definitely is. She lies more often than she tells the truth

On the other hand, Republicans, Conservatives, and Christians view Donald Trump so suspiciously that they abandon ship over trivial matters, saying they cannot support him. They are doing this despite knowing how important this election is. Although they agree with Trump about securing our borders, making us energy independent, strengthening the military, and appointing conservative Justices to the Supreme Court, they have become so easily offended that they are as fickle as a teenage cheerleader. This has to stop.

When Democrats show more intestinal fortitude than Republicans, Conservatives, and Christians, then you know we are in trouble. Folks, the future of our nation is at stake. It's time to grow a pair.

Mr. Trump, as I watch how the mainstream media has taken it upon themselves to "protect" us from you, I am amazed. Not one thing about you is being judged or reported on merit—not one thing. Instead, everything they say falls into a carefully crafted narrative, making you seem dangerous and reckless, which you are not, but your opponent, Hillary Clinton, is.

The media is projecting onto you Hillary Clinton's egregious character qualities—all in an attempt to uplift her by marginalizing you. Those of us who have the ability to discern the media's true motives understand what is happening, and we want to thank you for standing strong for us. America needs you at this critical hour of history. Hang in there, Donald, and be strong. In the long run, it will be worth it.

8/10

The Media's Goal Is to Marginalize Trump

RCP: Clinton – 48.0   Trump – 40.3

COMMON SENSE: During the Vietnam War, casualty figures were announced on Thursdays, including the number of enemy killed. Because there were so many enemy troops involved, the Tet Offensive in January 1968, came as a complete surprise. Because it was so massive, it quickly became apparent that the

Johnson Administration had been inflating the number of dead North Vietnamese for years. The outrage of the American people was so great that Johnson quickly withdrew from the Presidential race in 1968.

Now, we learn that the Obama administration has been doing exactly the same thing. Wanting us to believe that ISIS was "the J.V. Team" and not a serious threat, Team Obama, which includes Hillary, has purposefully deceived us.

In fact, it required a federal judge to compel the administration to tell the truth, which the administration fought tooth-n-nail.

Folks, we simply cannot continue to bury our heads in the sand about what is happening. It's time to get rid of this corrupt administration and not replace it with Obama 3.0, which is exactly what Hillary is offering us. If anything, she is more dishonest than President Obama. We simply must protect ourselves—period!

8/12

Trump Can't Win Saying Silly Things
RCP: Clinton – 47.5 Trump – 41.2

COMMON SENSE: Mr. Trump, your economic speech was excellent. Unfortunately, few paid any attention to it. Your entire agenda—all of which is essential to return America to greatness—was marginalized because of that one silly statement that was construed as being threatening to Hillary Clinton.

Sir, it's time to take the gloves off and get tough—not with Hillary but with yourself. You simply must stop allowing the news cycles to be about unimportant, off-the-cuff, ad hominem attacks that go over the top and alienate voters. You promised us that you would not "blow it" like Mitt Romney did four years ago, but that's exactly what you are doing.

There is so much coming out about Hillary's poor judgment and corruption that her supporters should be abandoning her candidacy in droves, but this isn't happening because of you. Each day, you are allowing the opposition—Hillary, her campaign, and the media—to paint you as an unsuitable alternative to her.

You simply must stop giving them ammunition to do this. If you can discipline yourself for three months, we might be able to save this great nation. If not, we will elect an unrepentant criminal to be our next President. The choice is yours, Mr. Trump, and so are the consequences.

8/12

Loretta Lynch Is as Corrupt as Hillary
RCP: Clinton – 47.5 Trump – 41.2

COMMON SENSE: Under oath, Attorney General Loretta Lynch testified to more than seventy questions, saying that she took the advice of the FBI concerning her decision not to indict Hillary Clinton. Lynch said this so many times it was clear that her intent was to stonewall Congress about Clinton's email server issue. For Lynch, the FBI was her cover for not doing her job

Now, we learn that at least three FBI Field Offices have requested authorization to investigate Hillary's pay-to-play scheme concerning her role as Secretary of State and donations given to the Clinton Foundation. What Hillary and her aides did, providing favors for donations, is criminal, and Lynch knows it.

Lynch wants it both ways. For one investigation, she relied on the FBI completely, but for the other, she has been unwilling to listen to the FBI. Something stinks here.

Lynch is corrupt. She has been compromised, and she has to go. Congress has it within its power to impeach her and make her stand trial for corruption, and our lawmakers need to do this. This entire Clinton State Department stinks to high Heaven, and the American people are tired of all of it.

The chant, "Lock her up," is appropriate for Hillary, but it is also the right one for Lynch. Our top cop is a crook.

8/13

Lord, Heal Our Land

RCP: Clinton – 47.8 Trump – 41.0

Father,
My heart aches and my spirit is grieved,

As I watch the systematic destruction of out great nation,
By those who took an oath to defend and protect us,
While they lead us in the exact opposite direction.

Haughty, arrogant, and corrupt, our leaders champion depravity,
Calling it noble, healthy, and the fulfillment of the American dream.
Reinterpreting history to suit their twisted, deceitful worldview,
They smile smugly at how successful they have become.

Father, there is so little that I can do to stand in their way.
I want to expose them and tell others how perilous the road ahead
Will be, but few are willing to listen or heed my warning.
Choosing to embrace deceitfulness over truth, they mock Your ways.

Will You hear my prayer, Lord? Will You intervene?
Will You move in a mighty way and spare or land,
Or have we traveled this foolish path for so long
That nothing but destruction and sorrow lie before us?

I do not have the answers, nor do I know the future.
All I can do is bow my knee before You and humbly
Beseech You to intervene and restore our nation
Before our self-serving ways devastate our future.

Amen

8/14

Why Wall Street Executives Favor Hillary

RCP: Clinton – 47.8 Trump – 41.0

COMMON SENSE: Why would Wall Street executives donate $49 million to Hillary's campaign and only $19 thousand to Trump's? What do they know that you may not know?

It's that our economy is so bad the Obama administration has had to inject $10 trillion into it in the last eight years, just to keep things going. It's why our National Debt has doubled. But how has Obama done this? Have you ever wondered?

He places it into the New York Stock Exchange. But, who benefits from this? The 1 percent does. Who gets screwed? You do—the middle class. Who understands this? The stockbrokers do, of course, and they don't want it to stop. So, when Obama and Hillary rail at the wealthiest Americans, they forget to tell you that their policies have funded the rich at the expense of hard-working Americans like you.

Essentially, we have maintained our standard of living by living on a credit card, incurring massive debt so that Obama and Hillary can fund entitlement programs that undermine American solvency.

Why hasn't anybody from the media bothered to tell you this? It's because they do not want you to know how badly you have been cheated. So, the next time Hillary or someone from the media holds up a Trump shirt and scolds him for having it manufactured overseas, remember that what they are really doing is deflecting from the real and substantive issue of Obama's and Hillary's deficit spending programs that will continue to make Wall Street executives filthy rich.

8/15

Trump Better on Energy Than Hillary
RCP: Clinton – 47.8 Trump – 41.0

COMMON SENSE: You have heard that OPEC nations, including Saudi Arabia, have given massive donations to the Clinton Foundation? But what does that mean and why is it important?

Trump is for the Keystone Pipeline, fracking, and deregulation of the energy industry. Hillary is opposed to all deregulation, including coal mining. Trump's goal is to make the USA energy independent, which he can do.

If Trump accomplishes this, and fails at every other thing he promises to do, his Presidency would be a roaring success. That's how important this issue is. This alone—energy independence—would return the Unites States to solvency.

If this is true, and it is, then why would Hillary be against it? The answer is simple. She is owned by Saudi Arabia and others—

bought and paid for with donations. They want to keep America dependent on them for oil. If Hillary wins, our $20 trillion in debt will increase. If Trump wins, and he is successful at turning energy production around, we will be great again. We will also be debt free soon.

On energy, the candidates are polar opposites, but not many have connected these dots. Being purposefully distracted on the issues, they simply do not understand what is happening or what is at stake. Anybody who does, however, will repudiate Hillary and vote for Trump.

8/17

Our Foreign Policy Needs to Change
RCP: Clinton – 47.2 Trump – 41.2

COMMON SENSE: World War II ended in August 1945. When it did, Germany and Japan were reduced to rubble. Pouring money and ideas into both nations, we began the arduous task of nation building, with surprising success. Both Germany and Japan embraced democracy and have become strong allies of the United States ever since. When the Korean War ended, we used the same strategy in South Korea, and they have also become a strong democracy and ally.

Having been so successful, the United States has maintained the conviction that we can win every war and successfully rebuild vanquished enemies into successful democracies, just like we did in Germany, Japan, and South Korea. As successful as that model was, it doesn't always work. In fact, it has never worked since. Yet, we keep trying to replicate it, despite having failed miserably in Indochina and the Middle East.

The reason we are no longer successful is we are trying to force our solution on people who don't want it, especially in the Middle East. People who want Sharia Law have nothing but contempt for constitutional democracy. Remember seeing the footage of people with a black thumb in Iraq, showing us they had voted? Although this made us feel good, it was an illusion. It seemed like we had won but we hadn't. That was an misperception as time has revealed.

We need to realize that our post World War II model no longer works. We cannot successfully impose our will on others. This was Bush 43's error and Obama's too. Instead, out of self-preservation, where political Islam is concerned, our policy should be one of containment. It's all we can do, but it's all we need to do to remain safe.

8/18

Hillary Is Completely Untrustworthy
RCP: Clinton – 47.0 Trump – 41,2

COMMON SENSE: Have you ever been in a relationship where

your partner questioned your fidelity, even though their misgivings were groundless? They were suspicious of everything you did, even the way you smiled at a complete stranger at the mall or at church. You found yourself having to explain and justify everything you did and thought. Have you ever been in a situation like this?

If you have, you may not have thought it through, but your partner was probably projecting onto you what he or she was actually doing. It was their way of justifying their duplicitous infidelity. Projection like this happens a lot.

It also occurs in politics. Take Hillary Clinton for example. Her charge that Donald Trump is "too reckless" to be trusted with the nuclear codes is groundless, but it's a projection about her own behavior. She repeats this charge wherever she goes, despite the fact that she is the one who the FBI has labeled "careless" about the way she handled classified material. Her negligence should have disqualified her, but it hasn't—thanks to the DOJ's fix.

Instead of being sorry, Hillary, aided by the media, has chosen to project her own egregious behavior onto Trump. She accuses him of the very thing about which she is guilty. Hillary is the one who cannot be trusted—not with anything. I base this conclusion solely on her past performance, which is the best predictor of future behavior.

8/20

Destroying Trump's Image Is the Media's Goal

RCP: Clinton – 47.0 Trump – 41.3

COMMON SENSE: It is immoral to support Donald J. Trump, according to the mainstream media. Only an ignorant bigot, someone devoid of compassion and basic human dignity, would even consider doing so. He is the champion of the ignorant, the vile, the uneducated, the obtuse, and nobody else. Worse, he definitely does not represent American values.

Relentlessly hammering this message home, reporters and anchors from the Left have been successful in their attempts to marginalize Donald Trump, painting the picture that he would be a destructive force for America. Unfortunately, some of Trump's missteps have helped make this picture more plausible. This message, brilliantly elucidated, has had one purpose—to ensure that Trump will never be President. To these Leftists, objectivity in reporting is not nearly as important as destroying Trump in the eyes of the American people.

At the same time, our "objective media" has not said a vote for Hillary Clinton should be the moral alternative. If any of them said this openly, because Hillary is deceitful and corrupt, which everybody knows, the media would lose their audience. Since she's the only alternative, however, it's obviously implied. It's never stated though, which is strategically brilliant. All they have needed to do is discredit Trump. Having done so, support for Hillary, although reluctant, would be the inevitable alternative.

The only thing standing in the way of the media's success is you. Are you smart enough to see through what they are doing? Are you wise enough to realize that their disapprobation of Trump has nothing to do with his policies? Are you plugged in enough to see that the media's criticisms of Trump are actually true of Hillary? If so, then we may still save our great nation from the manipulations of these amoral, reprehensible Sophists.

8/25

Hillary's Smoking Gun

RCP: Clinton – 48.3 Trump – 42.3

COMMON SENSE: Here is the "smoking gun" with Hillary. None of the emails she turned over to Congress or the FBI were related to the Clinton Foundation. She considered those email to be her personal business—like the one's involving Chelsea's wedding and yoga classes. This is her greatest vulnerability, and she knows it. Now that they are coming out, her house of cards may finally collapse, but I'm not holding my breath. The Queen of Corruption has more lives than Barbara Baird from the Moon Series.

8/25

Julian Assange Is a Hero –
Not a Villian

RCP: Clinton – 48.3 Trump – 42.3

COMMON SENSE: I disagree with most Conservatives about Julian Assange. I support his efforts to expose Hillary's emails. Here's why:

1. By not using a government server, as she promised she would, Hillary has brought all of this on herself with her own illegal, reckless behavior.

2. Since Bill Clinton cut a deal with Attorney General Loretta Lynch, which only a fool would deny, to keep the American people in the dark, Assange is our only hope of getting to the truth about Hillary's corruption before the election.

3. The FBI, which I used to believe was incorruptible, has proven to be no better than the DOJ. Both agencies have made her above the law.

4. If Assange doesn't post Hillary's emails and she wins in November, the Russians and Chinese, who have most certainly hacked Hillary's server, can use what they have on her to blackmail her into being as weak-willed as Obama. That we definitely cannot afford.

5. Since Hillary considered the emails about the Clinton Foun-

dation to be private, rather than having anything to do with State Department business, she did not include any of them in what she turned over. Thus, the evidence of her pay-to-play corruption is in those 14,900 that should have been made available to Congress and the FBI.

6. Since we can no longer trust our government to tell the truth, we must rely on others to do it. We have no other choice. Daniel Ellsberg was considered a hero for publishing *The Pentagon Papers*. He blew the whistle on President Nixon, and it was needed. I believe that what Assange has is necessary for the American people to know, and I believe he is just as heroic as Ellsberg.

8/26

OBAMA: Do Your Job – Prosecute Hillary

RCP: Clinton – 47.2 Trump – 41.8

COMMON SENSE: FBI Director Comey testified that there was "no intention" to deceive coming from Hillary Clinton, concerning her private email server. We now know this isn't true. Hillary did intend to deceive everybody about her activities from day one. By using the BleachBit program to hide her deleted emails, shredding them electronically, making them impossible to recover, Hillary's intentionality has been established.

We, the American people, cannot let this stand. Hillary Clinton needs to be prosecuted. President Obama needs to do his job, starting with the removal of Loretta Lynch and James Comey—both of whom have been compromised. If Obama refuses, Congress needs to step in. The level of corruption here is greater than Watergate. It needs to be ferreted out—period!

8/27

Trump Is Not a Racist – Shame on Hillary

RCP: Clinton – 48.4 Trump – 42.1

COMMON SENSE: Hillary Clinton is the reason why the Presidential Campaign is so negative—not Donald J. Trump. Because she cannot taut her record of accomplishment, failing miserably at everything she has ever done, especially at being our Secretary of State, all she can do is say, "Trump is more unsuitable than I am."

This is exactly what she is doing by calling Trump a racist, which he is not. If anything, the charge of racism could be levied at her, but I don't think it would be true, accurate or fair to do so. Her avowed mentor was Sen. Harry Byrd, who was a member of the Ku Klux Klan at one time. Bill Clinton's mentor was Sen. J. William Fulbright, also a member of the Klan. So, both Clintons do have a connection, although a thin one.

There is no historical record to indicate that Trump has ever had anything to do with the Ku Klux Klan, but Hillary is accusing him of being one of its supporters. A non-politician, Trump didn't even know who David Dukes was. Being a minor player, not many people know who he is.

Because Hillary is deceitful and corrupt, she has to do everything she can to put the spotlight on Trump, rather than answer uncomfortable questions about her pay-to-play scheme, where she used her position of authority to amass a fortune for her foundation. She should be in the jailhouse—not in the White House.

8/30

Hillary Is Corrupt by Nature – That Will Never Change

RCP: Clinton – 46.7 Trump – 41.7

COMMON SENSE: As more comes out about Hillary's corruption and pay-to-play scheme, requiring donations to her foundation before gaining access, I wonder what Barack Obama is thinking? Don't you?

He was her boss, but she not only lied to him, she also authorized her private server before she was even confirmed. This means she planed to be corrupt from day one. She didn't just drift into it, and her actions definitely will taint Obama's legacy.

Another thing to think about is this: If Hillary was this corrupt as

Secretary of State, when she had limited power, how corrupt will she be when her power is 100 times greater? If she lied to Obama about what she intended to do, what would make anybody think she's telling us the truth now? To take her at her word is ludicrous. Since past performance is the best indicator of future actions, we can count on Hillary to be deceitful, corrupt, and incompetent—nothing more, nothing less.

Trump's Black Outreach Has Merit
RCP: Clinton – 45.9 Trump – 42.3

COMMON SENSE: I love that Donald Trump went to Detroit, spoke at a black church, and visited the impoverished neighborhood that was once Dr. Ben Carson's home. Will it get him black votes? No, I doubt that it will, but I liked what he did anyway. It was the right thing to do.

Trump's idea to bring home American capital, tax free, if 10 percent of it is invested in inner city development projects, aimed at creating jobs, is brilliant. This would be a $2 trillion stimulus, which is huge. Plus, it's real money—not printed money that brings nothing other than inflation.

This is the kind of out-of-the-box thinking a successful businessman can do. By any standard, Trump's outreach was impressive, and so was his idea.

9/5

Putin Wants Hillary in Office – Not Trump

RCP: Clinton – 45.9 Trump – 42.3

COMMON SENSE: I just watched Hillary Clinton's abbreviated press conference on her plane, and I have two comments:

1. That it ended abruptly because Hillary was overtaken by a coughing fit indicates that she is physically unfit to do the job. She just isn't healthy enough to be President.

2. When she suggested that the Russians want Trump to win, you need to ask why that would be true? Putin is aggressive and has territorial aspirations in Eastern Europe. Who is more likely to stand in his way, Trump or Hillary? Neither Hillary nor Obama were willing to check Putin's annexation of the Crimea, were they? Also, if Putin has Hillary's deleted emails, he can blackmail her throughout her Presidency, which she knows. Instead of admitting how vulnerable this makes her, because she never admits anything, she is projecting her weakened position onto Trump. Keep this in mind because it's how Hillary plays the game.

9/8

Hillary "Needs Help Lying"
RCP: Clinton – 45.5 Trump – 42.8

COMMON SENSE: Ya gotta love Hillary! Just when you think there isn't any further low-down, devious, or sneaky thing she can do, she comes up with something new to surprises us.

In last night's semi-debate, she had a listening devise in her ear. This means that the "Most Qualified Person to Run for President" and "The Smartest Woman in the World" needed information to be fed to her to answer Matt Lauer's questions. Unbelievable!

There is nothing about Hillary that is straightforward and honest—not one thing. According to actor, James Wood, "She can't even lie without help." How can anyone take this woman seriously?

9/11

9/11 Unifies Us, Making Us Stronger
RCP: Clinton – 46.0 Trump – 42.9

COMMON SENSE: We all remember where we were and what we were doing, when we heard about the attack on 9/11. I was in a Barnes & Noble with with a friend, when his wife called, telling us about it. At first, it didn't seem plausible that we had been attacked. By the time the second tower was hit, I had returned home and saw it on TV.

Renewing my mind, from that moment forward, I have never altered my viewpoint or perspective. We were attacked by Radical Islamic Terrorists—by those who want to destroy us and our American way of life. To them, we are all the Great Satan—not just some of us.

On this day, let us remember we are Americans first and political opponents second. Many disagree with my worldview and I disagree with theirs. Nevertheless, none of us want to cut off each other's heads. That we can argue without killing each other is what makes us different, but it is also what makes us strong.

Remember, Jihadists have a sense of history, which makes every anniversary of 9/11 a particularly dangerous day for Americans, so be careful.

9/11

Hillary's Foundation Is a Massive Fraud

RCP: Clinton – 46.0 Trump – 42.9

COMMON SENSE: Concerning Hillary's email scandal, although having her own personal server and destroying evidence from it was criminal, this certainly isn't the most important issue. The greatest problem is why Hillary set it up in the first place.

It was the communications vehicle between her office as Secretary of State and the Clinton Foundation. She used the server to funnel large amounts of money to her Foundation.

Since its inception, there has never been an external audit of the Clinton Foundation, so nobody knows exactly how much money has been amassed or how deep her corruption goes. Suffice it to say, when the details of this pay-to-play scheme come out, which they will, Hillary will be featured in the Guinness Book of World Records for having accomplished the most massive fraud in world history.

9/13

Hillary Will Never Recover from 9/11 Episode

RCP: Clinton – 45.8 Trump – 43.4

COMMON SENSE: The way things are unfolding with Hillary Clinton's email scandal is exactly the way things unfolded with the Watergate scandal from 1972-74. At first, there was a story or two about the break in, but there was no momentum. This happened for quite some time, just like it is happening now.

Then, the momentum shifted, and an avalanche of stories became all-consuming, eventually forcing President Nixon to resign. The same scenario is unfolding—right before our eyes. I believe the video chip of Hillary collapsing is a perfect metaphor for what is about to happen.

Aided by the FBI and the DOJ, a shroud of secrecy has been established, in an attempt to cover-up Hillary's crimes, but their efforts will no longer be able to protect her. The pressure to reveal the truth has become too great.

When it becomes evident to Democrats running for office, that Hillary's criminality has become their problem, and may cost them their seats, they will abandon her.

Her destiny is set. She will never become President of the United States.

How appropriate that her undoing came on 9/11, four years to the day after she abandoned our brave men to die in Benghazi. Finally, justice for these men is about to happen.

9/18

It's Time to Deal with Terrorism Harshly

RCP: Clinton – 49.0 Trump – 44.0

COMMON SENSE: At this time four years ago, while lying about what was really behind the Benghazi attack, Obama's position was Osama bin Laden was dead, al Qaeda was on the run, and ISIS was the JV team. Believing Obama's false narrative to be true, Americans continued to deny reality by choosing the more politically correct position of toleration toward a worldview that is antithetical to ours.

We were wrong then and, if we choose Hillary's perpetuation of Obama's error, we will continue to be wrong. Even worse, we will sustain repeated attacks for the next four years. This is what will happen, whether you are willing to admit it is true or not.

In the past 24 hours, we have sustained attacks in Minnesota, New York, and New Jersey—all blue states. Radical Islamisists don't differentiate between the Right and Left. To them, we are all the Great Satan.

Isn't it time to stand up to these monsters? Isn't it time to abandon our false narrative and call things what they really are? Isn't it time to deal with these terrorists harshly and put an end to Radical Islamic Jihadism in America?

If your answer to these questions is yes, then you know what you need to do.

9/19

Hillary Is too Weak to Stop Terrorism
RCP: Clinton – 49.0 Trump – 44.0

COMMON SENSE: While CNN was busy deleting Hillary's use of the word "bomb" in her interview, after the attacks in New York

Saturday night—in an effort to make her look good and Trump look bad—the Jihadists were busy planning their next attack.

We have allowed the Trojan Horse of Radical Islam into our country, and we are going to pay a terrible price to get rid of it. Using the Internet, the "Cyber Islamic Army" is busy recruiting, indoctrinating, and sending out misguided fools to create havoc and carnage in America, while Obama is busy telling us how peaceful Islam is.

The time for submitting to this politically correct nonsense, at the expense of American lives, is over. We need new leadership, from people who are not corrupt, to forge the way forward. If we continue doing the same thing, which is Hillary's strategy, we will continue to get the same results. This tired, sick old woman cannot possibly do the job necessary to keep us safe. Trump has been consistently right on the issue of terrorism, and he is definitely strong enough to protect us. The choice is clear.

Email Server –
Hillary Obstructed Justice

RCP: Clinton – 45.3 Trump – 44.0

COMMON SENSE: Here is the "Smoking Gun" concerning Hillary's missing emails, and it definitely proves "intent," which the FBI says doesn't exist.

An army of Reddit users believes it has found evidence that former Hillary Clinton computer specialist, Paul Combetta, solicited free advice regarding Clinton's private email server from users of the popular web forum.

A collaborative investigation showed a Reddit user with the username "Stonetear" requested help in relation to retaining and purging email messages after 60 days, and requested advice on how to remove a "VERY VIP" individual's email address from archived content.

On July 23, 2014, the House Select Committee on Benghazi reached an agreement with the State Department on the production of records—Hillary's emails. It was the following day that "Stonetear" asked for help about how to take care of his problem. This constitutes Obstruction of Justice—a felony.

There is a massive cover-up here, with those perpetrating it fully intend to hand the election to Hillary. If they are successful, Hillary will do what she always does—destroy her enemies.

9/25

Hillary's Nature Is Untrustworthy
RCP: Clinton – 46.5 Trump – 43.4

COMMON SENSE: Hillary's surrogates, an ignoble lot, have been out doing the talk shows, saying she needs to work on being "trustworthy." This problem will never go away or even improve, and there's a reason why.

For Hillary, being trustworthy isn't part of her nature. At the core of who she is, she is deceitful. Lying is her default position. She always returns to it. So, no matter what she does—short of complete repentance—will not matter one bit. For her, working on the issue is trying to figure out what to say to make you think she is trustworthy—nothing else. Having been conned by her so frequently, only a few are still willing to take what she says at face value. Frankly, I'm impressed that her numbers in this area are in double digits.

9/26

Cruz Finally Endorses Trump
RCP: Clinton – 46.6 Trump – 44.3

COMMON SENSE: Many Conservatives are shocked and saddened by Ted Cruz's endorsement of Donald Trump. I'm not one of them. Neither do I believe it should have been a gut-wrenching decision for Cruz. He made a pledge to support the nominee, and he simply did what he committed to do.

Cruz promised us—the American people—that he would keep his pledge, and he made the commitment publicly. To not keep his pledge—like Kasich, Lindsay, and Jeb Bush—would have been dishonorable, and I would never have had anything to do with Cruz again.

Given the situation, I can see that he would feel angry about doing his duty. That's human and understandable, but to not do it at all would have revealed a character flaw that would disqualify him in the future.

No Republican has ever won the White House without winning Ohio, but Kasich will not lift a finger to prevent Hillary from winning his state. That he won't indicates his bitterness and personal ambition are more important to him than we are—the American people. I have no use for the man—period.

Keeping your word is a big deal for Conservatives and Christians. We can't help it. It's our nature to be high-minded—just like it's Hillary's nature to be corrupt and deceitful. Our candidate has flaws, but they are nothing like the depravity of Hillary and her team of amoral Sophists.

9/27

Why Trump Won the Debate
RCP: Clinton – 46.7 Trump – 44.3

COMMON SENSE: I remember the day after the 1980 Presidential Debate between Jimmy Carter and Ronald Reagan. When I went into the Political Science Department at Emory, where I was working on a Ph.D., all of the professors were ecstatic because they thought Jimmy Carter had "cleaned that cowboy's clock."

Being the only person in the department for Reagan, I was

crushed, but their glee turned out to be short lived. Within a few days, it was clear that Reagan had won. Although Carter's responses were more technically precise, he came across as unwarm and devoid of emotion. Reagan, by way of contrast, was genuine, warm, kind, and personable. Carter never recovered. The cowboy won, and we had the Reagan Revolution.

Last night, Hillary was technically on target, but she was also mean-spirited, smug, and unlikeable. Trump, by way of contrast, seemed like somebody you would like to have over for lunch.

Perhaps this is why the polls said he won the debate and Hillary didn't.

9/28

HILLARY: A Woman Without a Soul
RCP: Clinton – 47.4 Trump – 44.4

COMMON SENSE: I've read and watched the posts about how the Clinton Campaign rigged the Presidential Debate, and how Hillary and Lester Holt were complicit in a massive fraud. Considering all of the other scandals involving Hillary, I shouldn't be surprised by this, but I am—but not for the reason you might expect.

Hillary Clinton must have a terrible self-image and an extraordinarily low view of her competency. That she didn't believe she could beat Donald Trump is an honest, ethical debate—playing by the rules—speaks volumes. If she had any self-esteem, personal pride or dignity, she wouldn't have allowed such a thing to happen. If she was self-assured, she would have said, "I don't need any help. Bring Trump on, I can take him," but that's not what she did, is it?

She schemed to rig the system in her favor—just like she did to Bernie—revealing just how serious her dishonesty is. Because of this character flaw, the woman cannot play it straight no matter what.

Years ago, there was a great western, Maverick. The star, Bret, played by James Garner, made his living by gambling. The people he always liked to play poker with the most were cheaters. Once he knew their game, it was easy for him to beat them. It's the same with Hillary.

Other nations can't wait to get her elected, knowing just how easy it will be to manipulate such a weak person. Soulless and characterless, with her at our nation's helm, we will be in for some very serious troubles throughout the world. If you have kids or grandkids that are in high school, be nice to them because many may end up in body bags.

10/6

Putin Will Not Release Hillary's 33,000 Emails

RCP: Clinton – 44.8 Trump – 43.9

COMMON SENSE: Hillary is convinced Putin has intact versions of her 33,000 Bleach-Bitted emails, which certainly could destroy her. It's why she is doing everything in her power to tie Trump to Putin. Although this is a stretch, it's all she can do to mitigate the damage she believes is coming her way.

Conservatives and Trump supporters love this. They are counting on Putin releasing the emails before the election, handing the White House to Trump. Thinking it's their ace in the hole, they are counting on this.

If Putin has her 33,000 emails, which he may or may not, I doubt he will release them. The reason is simple. He's a Russian, looking out for Russian interests—not American interests. From his perspective, he would rather see Hillary win. Once she does, then he will release the emails, which are certain to destabilize the United States. That is in Russia's best interests—not helping Trump win.

If Putin can create a Constitutional crisis for us, by letting everybody know our President-Elect is definitely a crook and maybe a traitor, he will. Whatever weakens us, like having Obama or Hillary in the White House, is in his best interest. So, don't expect to see the emails before the election—not if Putin is the one who has them. Look for them shortly thereafter.

This Is How Trump Can Turn It Around

RCP: Clinton – 47.5 Trump – 42.9

COMMON SENSE: MR. TRUMP, If there was ever a time in your life to become humble, it is now—not just to say the right things, but to become the right things. Before the debate on Sunday night, on Sunday morning, you should get on your plane with Ben Carson and Mike Huckaby and just show up at that black church in Detroit—not to speak but to listen.

If you can do this, if you can hear the message, if you can repent of what has been debilitating you, if you can prostrate yourself before the Living God, then, and only then, can you redeem yourself with the American people.

Most of your supporters are people of faith. They are remarkably forgiving, but you have to give them something to work with that is substantial. Half measures will not work.

You need redemption. It can be yours, easily yours, but you have to allow the Holy Spirit to do a transforming work in you. If you can genuinely humble yourself, you will become empowered at a level beyond your capacity to understand, and you will become our next President.

Trump Is Standing Tall for the American People

RCP: Clinton – 47.9 Trump – 41.9

COMMON SENSE: Hillary Clinton has contempt for the Rule of law—shame on her. The Republican Establishment has equal contempt for the will of its party's voters—shame on the Republican Establishment.

My original candidate was Sen. Cruz. When he quit, I shifted to Trump. The Republican elites refuse to do this. Dan Senor, a Bush/Romney/Paul Ryan hack, is behind the audio clip aimed at derailing Donald Trump. This makes Senor a Quisling in my book. If Ryan had anything to do with this underhanded plot, he needs to resign as Speaker of the House.

When Trump went up against Hillary Sunday night, he was simultaneously fighting a coup from within his own party. Yet, he stood tall and soundly trounced the Queen of Corruption. Fighting for us, the American people, Trump was Presidential. I don't know about you, but I will proudly vote for him in November.

10/16

WikiLeaks Has Hillary and Obama Terrified

RCP: Clinton – 47.7 Trump – 42.2

COMMON SENSE: Hillary is terrified of being exposed by WikiLeaks—Obama too. They will do anything to divert attention away from the truth being revealed, including having a confrontation with Russia.

Think about how irresponsible their behavior is. It's like saying, "If I'm going down, I'm taking America down with me—perhaps Western Europe too."

Hillary and Obama tell us how dangerous it would be for Trump to have the nuclear codes, while at the same time, they are provoking a confrontation with Russia.

The tensions between the USA and Russia are the worst they have been since the Cuban Missile Crisis in 1962, and it's all because of Hillary and Barack trying to misdirect attention from the truth undermining their corruption. That so few recognize this for what it is, or are willing to speak out against such dereliction of duty, is astounding.

10/18

My Prayer for America

RCP: Clinton – 49.0 Trump – 41.9

PRAYER FOR AMERICA: Father,

My heart is heavy and deeply troubled.

I have a dreadful foreboding for the future.

After benefitting from the rewards of Your blessings

For generations, it seems like this may be the end.

Throughout our history, millions have honored You,

Acknowledging that You are the source of everything

Good and honorable that we have enjoyed,

But this is no longer true. As a people,

We no longer honor You or give thanks.

In fact, we do the exact opposite. Now, we are being led

By those who mock Your name—by those who champion

A way that is contrary to the ways of our forefathers.

In their devious hearts, these reprobates hold

Your people in contempt, calling us deplorable and irredeemable.

Championed by a modern-day Jezebel—a disgraceful, corrupt

And deceitful woman, who speaks with a serpentine tongue,

They legislate wrong and call it right, congratulating themselves

For being enlightened, but they are not. They are deceived,

Even persuading many of Your children to accept

The ways of darkness, calling them wise and beneficial.

We deserve the destruction that is about to fall upon us.
There can be no doubt about that, but in Your graciousness,
You can spare us from the reign of Jezebel. You are slow
To anger and quick to forgive. For the sake of those of us
Who have made a stand for You, please spare our nation—
Not because we deserve to be spared, which we do not,
But because of Your boundless lovingkindness,
Amen.

10/20

Hillary's Policies Will Create Confrontation with Russia

RCP: Clinton – 48.5 Trump – 42.1

COMMON SENSE: The most significance difference between Hillary and Trump will not be discussed by the mainstream media, but it may impact our lives more than all other differences put together.

It's the "No Fly Zone" over Syria and parts of Iraq. Hillary is committed to it; Trump thinks it's a bad idea. This is a critical policy difference. Hillary's position will create a military confrontation with Russia. She has already screwed up the Middle East. Now, she wants to make it worse—far worse.

Hillary says that Putin wants Trump to win. I suspect that's true, but it's probably because Putin doesn't want to have a war with the United States. No sane American wants to have war with Russia either.

Currently, the tensions between the United States and Russia are nearly as high as the Cuban Missile Crisis in 1962, and it's because of how poorly Obama and Hillary have handled the Middle East and Eastern Europe. The reckless candidate is not Donald Trump; it's Hillary Clinton.

10/28

The Clintons Are Completely Corrupt
RCP: Clinton – 47.1 Trump – 41.5

COMMON SENSE: At first, the stories about the corruption of the Clintons were just a trickle. Now, these stories have become a steady stream. Soon, within days, they will become a flood, but the moral outrage about Bill and Hillary's behavior has been tepid at best, even among many misguided people of faith.

Since when has political corruption been morally acceptable? Since when has our leader, the President of the United States, sided with the corrupt at the expense of the American people? Since when has the FBI, allegedly the premier law enforcement agency in the world, given a pass to criminals, choosing personal gain for themselves instead? Since when has our media, who are supposed to seek the truth, been more invested in obscuring reality?

For too long, the American people have been passive but no longer. We are rising up in righteous indignation to hold these crooks accountable. Their time for reckoning is at hand.

11/3

I Believe Iran Hacked Hillary's Email Server

RCP: Clinton – 46.6 Trump – 45.3

COMMON SENSE: Last summer, we were told that no foreign governments hacked into Hillary's email server. We now know that was a lie. At least five nations have, and I believe one of them was Iran. If I'm right, and the evidence indicates that I am, it explains a lot.

Because the Obama administration does not want the contents of Hillary's server to be revealed, going to great lengths to aid her in a cover up, it has been easy for Iran to blackmail the United States. It explains why we lifted economic sanctions on Iran and gave them $1.7 billion, including at least $400 million in cash. It also explains why our Attorney General, Loretta Lynch, would take the 5th about her involvement in this disastrous one-way, criminally negligent deal.

It also provides insight into why we have signed a disastrous deal that will lead Iran to develop nuclear weapons in less than five years. Maintaining the cover up has been so important that we have put Israel's existence at risk. It's also why Iran can buzz our Navy without fear of reprisal and why they can capture our sailors with no fear of reprisal. Secretary of State Kerry even thanked Iran for treating our sailors well, which the photo flatly contradicts.

What are Hillary and the Obama administration so intent on hiding? The FBI has the answers and so does the NYPD. It's also why our corrupt Department of Justice is so intent on squashing the investigation into the server and the Clinton Foundation. We need answers, and we need them now.

11/5

Hillary's Corruption Explained
RCP: Clinton – 46.5 Trump – 45.0

COMMON SENSE: Concerning the criminal investigations into Hillary's conduct, I want to connect the dots so that it's easier to understand exactly what is happening.

The investigation into her emails and the unauthorized server is simple. She sent classified information illegally, and each time she did this was a crime. For what she did, lesser mortals would spend the rest of their lives in Leavenworth, but certainly not Hillary. This wasn't done for convenience though. The purpose of the server was far more sinister, leading to the greater problem.

As Secretary of State, all of her communications belong to the

American people, making everything she did subject to Freedom of Information requests. Because of what she planned to do, she couldn't allow her communications to become public knowledge, so her private server became necessary. It was the way she and her surrogates communicated with the Clinton Foundation, Clinton Global Initiative, and Bill Clinton, Inc.

It was an elaborate scheme to use her position of trust to make Bill and her fabulously rich, which they now are. Essentially, she sold her influence to foreign governments and powerful business interests for money. It was a pay-to-play enterprise that was extraordinarily successful for her, and it all came at the expense of the American people. It was a criminal conspiracy from day one, and billions of dollars ran through the Clinton Foundation, all disguised as charity.

To get away with this, she had to corrupt a legion of people in government service, which she has done. As Secretary of State, she has done all of this. Heaven help us if she is elected President.

Our Destiny Is in God's Hands
RCP: Clinton – 47.0 Trump – 43.8

COMMON SENSE: We wanted either WikiLeaks or Anonymous to have made our job easier. Maybe they have and we just don't realize it. We didn't get what we expected, but we may have obtained what we need.

We now know exactly what Team Clinton is. It has become crystal clear. They are far worse than anything we ever imagined. By learning about Spirit Cooking and all of Hillary's schemes to arm our enemies, while enriching herself, there is no gray area about any of the goals these depraved people have.

Our goal is to take our nation back from those who will destroy it—nothing more, nothing less. The United States has been in the hands of the corrupt special interests and their bureaucratic henchmen for too long. Trump says we need to "Drain the Swamp." He's right, but there is also a spiritual battle that is raging. Everything may be against us, but the Lord certainly isn't, despite what some jaded, cynical Christians have to say.

Unapologetically, we stand in the tradition of our Forefathers. We intend to keep the faith; remain strong; and be ever vigilant. Our cause is just and the outcome is in the hands of Almighty God— not in the hands of the damnable god of Spirit Cooking.

11/9

MY PRAYER:
Thank You, Almighty God

Electorial College: Clinton – 232 Trump – 306

MY PRAYER: Father,

You have been so gracious to us,

Answering our deep heartache

In a way that cannot be denied.

In Your mercy and goodness,

You have spared us from the destruction

Of those who mock Your name

And champion darkness and depravity.

Thank you, Father, for intervening

And for giving us another chance to be

The people You have called us to me.

By answering our prayers, You have provided us

With the opportunity to walk in the light,

Free from the constraints of those who mock You

And support the evil of this world's god.

Now that we have bowed our collective knees to You,

Give us the wisdom and courage to stand and move forward,

Championing the rights of all, including the unborn.

Give us the strength to stand firmly against those

Who hate You and Your ways. Let us be kind

And forgiving, while making certain to hold each citizen
Accountable to the Rule of Law, regardless of who they are.

You still have a purpose for the United States of America,
And we humbly ask You to make Your will known to us.
Your mercy and graciousness are boundless.
On this day, when righteousness has been victorious,
We want to acknowledge You as the Author
Of our great victory over the arrogantly corrupt.
Without Your active intervention, all would have been lost.
We know this; help us to never forget it,
Amen

Conclusion

We have achieved a great victory; there's no question about it. Normally, one might think about Trump's accomplisment like winning the Super Bowl. Once victory in the football game has been achieved, that's the end of the season. Once your team has been crowned the champion, your life returns to normal, and you go back to other things until the following season.

This is precisely how most of Trump's supporters think about politics, but this is a serious mistake. We simply cannot afford to "return to normal." There is too much to do, and the stakes are too high.

Yes, we won, but all we have achieved is the opportunity to turn this nation around, nothing more. Continuing with my Super Bowl analogy, it's much better to conceptualize our victory as being one touchdown ahead at the end of the first quarter than to think the game is over. Knowing we are in a colossal battle between adherence to the faith of our Forefathers or embracing the godlessness of Progressivism, it will take a great deal of effort to actually win the game.

Although Trump is now President, we are still in debt by $20 trillion, half of which has come from Obama. Our infrastructure is a mess. The Middle East is more unstable than ever, and the wall separating the United States and Mexico needs to become a reality.

Many things need to happen, and every one of them is critical. Although there are many pressing issues, in my opinion, the campaign promise that is the most important is "Draining the Swamp." There's a good reason why I believe this, and it has nothing to do with being vengeful toward Hillary Clinton or the Obama administration.

The Progressives have suffered a great defeat, but they still believe in their cause. Their goal is to remold the United States into a Socialist democracy like those found in Western Europe. Their vision for our nation's future has not changed, and they will work twice as hard in 2020 to elect a President who fits into the mold of President Obama. This is their goal—make no mistake about it.

Despite Hillary's defeat, the Progressives continue to believe in their dream for the future. They are committed to retaking the White House. They also continue to believe in the integrity of their leaders, but this is an illusion. In reality, many of their leaders have been deeply corrupted.

This is what "Draining the Swamp" is all about, and it absolutely must be done. By exposing the deeds of darkness of President Obama, Secretary of State Hillary Clinton, and numerous others, this will demonstrate exactly how nefarious the purposes of the Progressives are.

Progressivism isn't just an alternative worldview. It's far more sinister than this. Progressivism is the philosophical mortal enemy of everything most of Trump's supporters hold dear. To head us in the right direction, it isn't enough to simply win elections. We must be engaged in changing the hearts and minds of millions of our fellow citizens—those who have been deceived by Progressivism's false message.

This will not be an easy task, but it must be done. Each dishonest and reprehensible deed of Hillary's must be brought to the light, especially those revealing her moral depravity—Obama's too. When everything is revealed and becomes evident to the rank and file Progressive, the sheer number of corrupt acts will be disheartening to millions of Progressives, and they will abandon its cause.

Realizing the heroes and heroines of their flawed belief system have been in it for themselves and not for the "noble cause," many will repudiate the false nobility of Progressivism's messengers. This will adversely impact the ability of this damnable worldview to win elections for years, perhaps forever.

Just as important, "Draining the Swamp" will continue to erode the credibility of the mainstream media, nearly all of whom have soft peddled the corruption of Hillary Clinton's pay-to-play foundation, as well as the excesses of the Obama administration.

Immediately after our victory in the Presidential Election, I wrote several posts about the importance of "Draining the Swamp." Because they were so well received by my Facebook friends, I have included them as well.

POST ELECTION 1

Hold the Obama Administration Accountable

COMMON SENSE: Of all of Trump's promises that need to be fulfilled, none is more important than "Draining the Swamp," but I can assure you this is the least appealing campaign promise to the Obama administration. They will do anything to keep from being exposed, which is exactly why it needs to happen.

The State Department, Department of Justice, Veterans Administration, Environmental Protection Agency, and Internal Revenue Service are good places to start. We have been led by thieves who have amassed personal fortunes—all at the expense of hard-working Americans like you and me. Now it's time that their deeds of darkness become exposed to the light.

Obviously, they will not like this. We will be called vengeful, but this is not true. We simply insist that they be held accountable and brought to justice. If Obama chooses to pardon them, then we will know just how deeply he has been involved in what happened during his watch.

POST ELECTION 2

Draining the Swamp
Must Be a Priority

COMMON SENSE: There will be tremendous opposition to "Draining the Swamp," particularly from the mainstream media. They will say that it goes against the traditions of our democracy to criminalize the behavior of our political opponents. Normally, this would be true, but not this time. People went to jail after Watergate, and they needs to go to jail this time as well.

The level of dishonesty is too great to ignore in the Obama administration. Believing they would never be held accountable, a culture of corruption has become the norm in our nation's capitol and not the exception. Beginning with Loretta Lynch, the Attorney General, Jeff Sessions, needs to investigate everything concerning the massive corruption that has been happening during the Obama administration. Each deed of darkness needs to be exposed to the light so that every Progressive, Leftist, and "useful fool" can see exactly who has become rich by stealing from the American people. This is not a time for mercy; it's a time for accountability.

POST ELECTION 3

Investigating the Clinton Foundation Must Continue

COMMON SENSE: Many have advocated the abandonment of investigating the Clinton Foundation. They say, "Why dwell on the past, when there is so much to do to make America great again?"

Nonsense! Let me explain why that is a bad idea and we cannot allow it to happen.

First, President Trump promised to "Drain the Swamp," and he must hold true to his word.

Second, the Rule of Law, which has been abandoned by the Obama administration, must be restored. The corrupt must be held accountable for their crimes, and the fortunes they have amassed illegally must be returned to the American people.

Third, by Draining the Swamp for the world to see, the false god of Statism will be dealt a substantial blow. The elites in government, the media, and academia have been entertaining themselves for decades in a massive circle jerk of deception, gleefully mocking all who are beneath them—deplorables like you and me. It's time to expose this false ruling class for the frauds they are, which will happen with the unmasking of Hillary Clinton.

Let a Special Prosecutor be appointed. When the truth is revealed, millennials by the millions will abandon the false beliefs of Progressivism. This will happen, believe me.

The Criminal Investigation Must Continue No Matter What

COMMON SENSE: Our goal cannot simply be to change Barack Obama's policies. We must do more than this—much more.

To kill Dracula, you must pound a stake through his heart. To destroy the godlessness of Progressive ideology, we must expose it for exactly what it is. The way to do this is to "Drain the Swamp," even if Obama pardons most of the criminals from his administration—people like Hillary Clinton, Loretta Lynch, and John Koskinen.

The investigations must move forward. The American people, especially Progressive Millennials, must be made aware of exactly who their champions are. The deeds of darkness of these miscreants must be exposed to the light. When this happens, many impressionable young people will realize exactly how badly they have been deceived.

To make America great again, we must return to the values of our Forefathers. Nothing less will work long-term. To get the job done, we must pound a stake into the heart of Progressive ideology, which is antithetical to core American values.

POST ELECTION 5

The Mainstream Media Is the Big Loser

COMMON SENSE: In my opinion, the greatest loser in the last election is the mainstream media. It's not just that they were wrong in predicting the outcome. It goes much deeper than that.

Essentially, by skewing the news to fit the narrative they wanted us to accept, they bet their future on the outcome. Now that their Progressive worldview has been soundly repudiated by patriotic populism, all they have left is their bitter vitriol to a populace that no longer pays attention—not the way they once did anyway.

In the years ahead, with diminished viewership, which means loss of advertising revenue, many of these journalists will be forced out of their jobs and end up teaching at universities. It's inevitable.

Do I feel sorry for them? No, I do not. I feel sorry for the impressionable kids at the universities who will be infected by the false belief system of these Leftist Progressives.

POST ELECTION 6

Hillary's Investigation Must Continue

COMMON SENSE: There are good and substantial reasons to pursue the criminal investigation into the Clinton Foundation, Clinton Global Initiative, and Bill Clinton Inc. Right now, people on both sides have emotional reactions about the Clintons, but nobody has the complete facts, which everyone needs for full disclosure.

To reestablish confidence in the Rule of Law, where everyone is held equally accountable, the investigation must go forward. To "Drain the Swamp," the investigation must continue. Nobody knows how far-reaching the tentacles of Hillary's corruption goes, but we must learn. To simply let it slide, while allowing the Clintons to enjoy the fruits of their ill-gotten gains, is an unacceptable outcome.

To assert that Hillary has suffered enough is ridiculous. She hasn't suffered at all, nor has she been held accountable for her actions—not ever. When the truth is finally revealed, it will be a major blow to Progressives and to the mainstream media. Once they learn they have championed a career criminal, there will be massive soul searching by the Progressive elites who believe they are wiser than the rest of us. Numerous college students will have to face uncomfortable facts.

All of this is necessary to move forward, and none of it is vengeful. It's just pursuing the truth. It's the responsibility of Congress and Trump's Attorney General to see that justice is served, and we must hold their feet to the fire. We will accept nothing less than a thorough investigation—period.

The previous six posts were all aimed at explaining why "Draining the Swamp" is necessary. Even when this has been accomplished, we will have barely begun to take our nation back, but it's a good start.

To be successful, we must have the attitude that our work has just begun. To be sure, there is a lot to do, but it's enjoyable work and very fulfilling. It will take years, which means it's time to roll up our sleeves and get busy.

Just think of it, we now have the opportunity to make America great again and to provide the following generation of Americans with a solid foundation.

—Jack Watts